T0113908

Messages Through *the* Ages

Jean Melson

WESTBOW
PRESS®
A DIVISION OF THOMAS NELSON
& ZONDERVAN

WestBow Press books may be ordered through booksellers or by contacting:

WestBow Press
A Division of Thomas Nelson & Zondervan
1663 Liberty Drive
Bloomington, IN 47403
www.westbowpress.com
844-714-3454

Scripture taken from the New King James Version® Copyright © 1982 by Thomas Nelson. Used by permission. All rights reserved.

ISBN: 978-1-6642-5307-0 (sc)
ISBN: 978-1-6642-5306-3 (e)

Print information available on the last page.

WestBow Press rev. date: 1/22/2022

CONTENTS

FOREWORD

I was one of the lucky ones. I grew up in a small town with loving parents, grandparents, great-grandparents, aunts and uncles, great-aunts and uncles, Bible class teachers and neighbor ladies. Everybody in our community knew my family and each of these women helped raise me. (Sometimes it took several to get the job done.)

Now, as I look back over my life, I can hear again, their messages. If I listen, I can still hear their voices, see the love in their eyes or the stern look of their mouth. I can hear their warnings. My mother would say, "We've already talked about this!" I can still hear Mamo say, "Jean! Just stop a minute and think!" They would encourage me and congratulate me on a job well done. My mother's sister taught me how to roller skate, and I can still here her say, "You were born to do this! Just keep going!" She was right. Years later, some friends and I opened a skating rink!

I can hear them reading with me, helping me with memory verses, the multiplication tables and spelling words.

There are times I still need their words of instruction, correction and encouragement. I wonder what advice or instruction they would have if they knew I was writing books?

There are other women, from long ago, who left messages for us. Messages to help raise us up to be children of God.

Open your Bible with me. Envision the women of long ago. Walk with me through their lives and listen. Can you hear their messages coming through the ages?

DEDICATION

This book is dedicated to my mother, Edna Bayliss (Mom), my grandmother, Hallie Bayliss (Mamo) and my great-grandmother Hulda Donze (Grandma).

All three of these women were faithful Christians. They loved the Lord and they loved me enough to teach me what was right and correct me when I was wrong. It wasn't always what I wanted to hear at the time.

I wish I could go back in time and tell them what I have discovered: Every time I didn't like what you told me......you were always right!

You all have received your promised, heavenly reward and if it were possible for the heavenly beings to deliver to you a message from me, it would be: Thank you! Thank you for never giving up on me! Thank you for loving me! I am doing my very best, to come see you one day!

AND, that is my message to Heavenly Father as well!

THANK YOU

A great big "Thank you" to two people, without whom, this book would not have been published.

"Thank you" Mike, my wonderful husband, for your love, your encouragement and patience. Sometimes I got so caught up in my study and writing, I let other duties slide and you were there to encourage me and help me.

"Thank you" to my good friend and sometimes secretary, Kay Johnson. I typed the manuscript and she did the rest, because when I sit at a computer, chaos and disaster happen. (and a belated thank you, Kay, for all your help with the first book!)

And another big "Thank you" to all of you who bought my first book, "Remembering God and Reminding Others" and to you who will buy this one. All royalties from both books are divided between the mission work of the Village Church of Christ and Jackson House in Hot Springs, a place where Mike and I volunteer to help feed the needy.

Buy some more!

BEFORE WE GET STARTED

Was the Bible written by men, to men and for men? Do these ancient writings have anything to do with me, a woman? Does this book include examples, instructions and expectations for me also?

From the very beginning, God's plan included women. There has always been a place for us; a purpose, a work and a reward.

The Bible is filled with wonderful, courageous, intelligent talented, obedient, faithful women! Their examples and messages have been recorded and handed down through the generations, for the purpose of inspiring us to be loving, true, faithful followers of God. Do we hear their messages?

King Solomon was the third king of Israel and son of King David. We read in 1Kings 3:7-14, God gave Solomon a miraculous measure of understanding and wisdom. He wrote three thousand proverbs (guides for living) and more than a thousand songs of beauty, inspiration and encouragement.

(1 Kings 4:32) Using this wisdom, he had some things to say to us. Stop here and open your Bibles and read with me, Proverbs 31:10-31.

Some of you say: That isn't me! I'm not married. I don't live in a household like that. I'm too young. I'm too old.

Did you miss the message?!? These verses describe a woman living a life of virtue: a life of goodness, righteousness, decency and moral principles. No matter what age or circumstances.

She has a good heart. She is a hard worker; she is not lazy. She is a good business woman. She provides for herself, her family and the poor. She plans ahead, she doesn't "put things off till tomorrow". She takes pride in the appearance of herself and her family. She is a person of strength, faith and honor. She is a happy woman full of hope. She is wise and kind. She fears the Lord and is known for her good works.

Does this remind you of what Paul wrote to the church in Galatia? The fruit of the Spirit is: love, joy, peace, patience, kindness, goodness, faithfulness, gentleness and self control. (Galatians 5:22-23)

Solomon also tells us what the ungodly, wicked, immoral, foolish woman looks like. (Proverbs 5:3-8, 7:10-27, 9:13-18)

The book of 1Kings is an inspired book of history, thought to have been written by the prophet, Jeremiah. Read 1Kings 11:1-13. This passage paints a clear picture of the destructive influence an ungodly woman can have over a man. Even a man with a good heart, full of wisdom. A man who loved God! A man to whom the One True God had spoken! Not once but three times! (1Kings 3:5, 9:2, 11:11) This man, full of wisdom, turned against God and lost his kingdom! It became a divided kingdom, ruled by wicked men, each more wicked than the last. Why? Because King Solomon allowed ungodly women to turn his heart from God! These women brought about the fall of the kingdom of Israel! And it was never completely restored.

Ever.

If someone were to record your story, what would you look like? Whatever your age; teen, unmarried, married, mother, grandmother. How would you be described?

When I was a kid, we had a neighbor woman, old enough to be my grandmother and she was mean! She just didn't like kids or anyone else. I asked my great grandma why some old ladies were so mean and others were so sweet. This was her answer: If a woman is mean at 70, she was devious at 50. If she was devious at 50, she was hard to get along with at 30. If she was hard to get along with at 30, she was selfish and unruly at 20. If she was selfish and unruly at 20, she was a brat at 10!

How did you start out? What do you look like now? It is never to late to change; to study, to learn, to prepare, to leave a different message. With God's help, your life can be a message of love, filled with the gifts of the Holy Spirit.

We are going to open our Bibles and look for the messages some of the women have left for us.

But first..... Who are all these people?

The Bible can sometimes be like a giant jigsaw puzzle. In order to see the whole picture, you need to put all the pieces together.

To prove who Jesus is, we read all the prophecies about Him in the Old Testament. Then we read about those prophesies coming true in the New Testament. Any one of those prophecies could be true about a hundred or even a thousand men, but all the prophesies fit only one man, Jesus the Christ.

The people we read about in the first four books of the New Testament can sometimes be really confusing; so many of them had common names like Mary, John or James. And to really muddy the water, a lot of them went by two names or more, because they were of Jewish (Hebrew) ancestry living in a Greek society. And to make matters worse, there may have been more than one way to spell the same name!

Many of these people were related. Family connections, which, when you think about it, really makes sense. The story of Jesus begins with family connections! Jewish people had strong family ties and Jesus grew up, like some of us, with aunts, uncles and cousins, many sharing the same family name or family business.

Is it important for us to know who they are? Do we need to know their connections and relationships to each other and to Jesus? Part of our problem is, the men who wrote these books and letters of the New Testament, knew all these people and the people they were writing to either knew them too or knew about them, so the connections were not always explained.

For example: A woman named Nancy has a sister named Rebekah,(Becky) and two daughters named Jamie Lee and Patricia (Pat). Now, you know the family. So...do you say...

Lee, the daughter of Becky's sister, Nancy, is going to visit her sister, Patricia. Or do you say: Jamie is going to visit her sister.

In the four books of Gospel, there are four writers giving their account of what they saw and heard. Everything each man wrote was inspired truth! But, each man tells different details about what he saw and heard.

Is it too confusing? Do we need to know? Sometimes we do need to know. For instance, many people think James, the brother of Jesus was one of the twelve apostles. Not so. When Jesus chose His apostles, (Luke 6:12-16) there were three James' listed.

1. James the son of Alphaeus.
2. James, the brother of John, sons of Zebedee.
3. One of the apostles has a father named James. We don't know anymore about this James.

None of these Jameses were the brother of Jesus.

Now lets talk about the Marys of the New Testament.

Mary is the Greek form of the Hebrew, Miriam and was a very common name. Let's begin with the Marys found at the crucifixion of Christ. Matthew (27:56), Mark (15:40) and John (19:25) each name three Marys at the foot of the cross. Luke does not name any of the women there.

The FIRST Mary is the mother of Jesus. Mathew (13:55-56) and Mark(6:3) tell us this Mary had five sons and at least two daughters. Jesus, James, Joses, Judas, sometimes called Jude and Simon. The girls are not named.

In Matthew's account, He called her the mother of James and Joses.

In Mark's account, he called her the mother of James the Less. Now you know, James the Less was not an apostle.

John called her the mother of Jesus.

The SECOND Mary is Mary Magdalene. All three men mention her by name.

The THIRD Mary, John said was the wife of Clopas. Matthew called her the other Mary. Clopas is believed to be the same man Jesus appeared to on the road to Emmaus after His resurrection. Luke spelled his name Cleopas. (Luke 24:18)

In addition to the three Marys at the cross, there is a FOURTH Mary. Mary of Bethany, sister of Martha.

The FIFTH Mary is Mary of Rome. She was a member of the church in Rome.

The SIXTH Mary is the mother of John Mark, the writer of one of the four books of gospel.

So far we have only introduced these Marys. We will go into a deeper study of some of them later, along with many other women. All kinds of women. All kinds of stories.

Open your Bible with me and lets walk through their lives and listen for their messages.

SIDE NOTE There is a song suggested at the end of each story. If you don't have hymn books in your home, look for the songs on line. It will be well worth your while to read these beautiful words over and over and hear the wonderful messages.

CHAPTER ONE

EVE

Genesis 1-5

The book of Genesis covers a lot of years in just a few pages. Time from the days of creation until Adam and Eve were put out of the garden is unknowable. After they left the garden, it was about twenty five hundred years until Noah was born. All that history in just five chapters! About 20 minutes of reading time.

The story of the creation of Adam and Eve is told twice in the first two chapters. We are told God created the heavens and the earth, sun, stars, fish, birds and animals. But none of those things were created in His image, His likeness. Only man and woman were created in His image. **In the day that God created man, He made them in the likeness of God, He created them male and female, and blessed them and called them Mankind in the day they were created.** (Genesis 5:1-2)

What does it mean to be created in His image? To be created with an everlasting soul. All the earth and everything in it will come to an end, even the bodies of Mankind. But the soul of man, like God, will never die. Genesis 35:18 Matthew10:28

1

And God created Adam and Eve and put them in a garden prepared especially for them. A perfect place. How long were they in the garden? Ten years? A thousand years? We don't know, but When God created them, He told them to be fruitful and multiply, just like He told the sea creatures and birds to multiply.(Genesis1:22,28) And God gave Adam work to do; he was to tend the garden and name the birds and animals But the best part of being in the garden was talking and walking with God!

Adam and Eve were also created with a will of their own. All the time they were in the garden, they chose to obey the command of God. **Of every tree in the garden you may freely eat, but of the tree of the knowledge of good and evil you shall not eat, for in the day that you eat of it you shall surely die.** (Genesis 2:16-17)

And then one day she had a visitor; Satan in the form of a serpent. What he looked like we don't know, but it was not what we think of as a snake. He was not crawling or slithering on the ground. And he was not of a threatening appearance. That would later be his curse for the part he played in what happened next.

When Satan spoke with Eve, he did what he always does, he lied! Five thousand years later, Jesus would say, speaking of Satan, **When he speaks a lie, he speaks from his own resources, for he is a liar and the father of it.** (John 8:44)

That is Satan's greatest weapon. He asked Eve if she could eat of every tree and she replied of every tree we may eat but one, if we eat of that one, we will die. Listen to what Satan said to her, **You will not surly die. God knows that the day you eat of it your eyes will be opened and you will be like God, knowing good and evil.** (Genesis 3:4,5)

Read it again. Everything he said was true except one word! NOT Everything else was true! That is Satan's most effective device; hiding a deadly lie in a truth. Making the truth a lie.

And Eve believed the lie and that led to her disobeying God and eating of the fruit. And that led to the end of her life as she knew it. Nothing would ever be the same again. From that moment on, her body began to age (admittedly, it took more than 900 years). Then she gave the fruit to Adam, with the same result.

And they were put out of the garden! Never again to walk in the cool of the evening and talk with God! So it was a spiritual death as well as a physical death. And there was more to the curse!

Satan was cursed to crawl on his belly for his part in this. Adam's curse, would be hard labor for the rest of his life. Never again the pleasant tasks he enjoyed in the garden.

As for Eve, her curse was three fold. **I will greatly multiply your sorrow and your conception; in pain you will bring forth children; Your desire shall be for your husband, And he shall rule over you.** (Genesis 3:16)

When we read the next chapter, several years have passed and she had given birth to two sons. The two men had a conflict over how to serve and obey God and it got so bad, Cain killed his only sibling, Able. Cain had to leave home. He went to the land of Nod and there he found a wife and built a life. We are told Eve is the mother of all living. (Genesis 3:20). The people of Nod had to be her offspring while she was in the garden! That is the answer to the first part of the curse. Until she was put out of the garden, childbirth had been painless!

The second part of her curse would be sexual desire. Until the curse, these two people were absolutely innocent! There was no desire, because desire itself brings pain, anxiety, jealousy and temptation. They evidently mated, as God instructed them (Genesis1:7-8) but now they would look at one another in a different way. Desire was something they would need to learn to control; they never needed self control before.

The third part of her curse put her in subjection to her husband. Their new circumstances would require a lot of decision making. Now Adam would need to step up and be the provider, protector and companion, and Eve would need to allow him that roll in her life. Now, for the first time, they would have a difference of opinion! What to do and how to do! Someone would have the final say and God said man would be the head of the house!

Eve and her husband had their third son after they had been out of the garden a hundred and thirty years and they named him Seth. (Genesis 4:25-26) After the birth of Seth, they lived another eight hundred years and had sons and daughters. Adam died at nine hundred thirty years of age. We are not told how old Eve was when she died, But she did, just as God said she would.

We are never told one word she said or one thought she had after she left the garden. Her life sounds pretty grim, doesn't it? God gave her a job to do and she did it. She had children and populated the earth.

Five thousand years later, Paul would write to Timothy about Eve and tell him, if she had children and they,(Adam and Eve), **continued in faith, love, holiness and self control** (all the things needed to combat the curse) **she will be saved.** (1 Timothy 2:13-15)

Is Eve sending us a message? What is it?

Listen to God. Know the truth. Recognize a lie and don't believe it! **If you abide in My word, you are My disciples indeed. And you shall know the truth and the truth shall set you free.** (John 8:31-32)

FOOD FOR THOUGHT

1. What was the immediate result of Eve believing the lie?
   Genesis 3:4-16

2. What was the far reaching result?
   Genesis 6:5-7
   1 Corinthians 15:21-22 NKJV

3. Is it our responsibility to know if something is a lie, or can we say
   "I just didn't know"?
   Acts 17:11,30

4. Are we to compare what someone tells us to what the Bible says? Or
   do we trust them to tell us the truth?
   2 Timothy 2:14-17

5. Do you ever go for a walk, just you and your Heavenly Father? Walk
   through His creation, see the beauty around you and just spend
   time with Him, like Eve used to do?

SONG   MY GOD AND I

CHAPTER 2

MRS. JOB

the Book of Job

After the flood, the sons of Noah began to repopulate the earth. (Genesis 9:19) Four hundred years later, Abraham was born. (Genesis 11:27)

Somewhere just before Abraham, Job and his wife lived in the land of Uz. They were a family of herdsmen with over fifteen hundred head of stock animals and a very large household (family, servants, herdsmen and their families). They were not nomads, they lived in houses. Think: large Texas ranch. He was the richest man in the East. Mrs Job lacked nothing! And she had seven sons and three daughters. Her life was wonderful!

The very best thing she had was a husband **that was blameless and upright, and one who feared God and shunned evil. He would rise early in the morning and offer burnt offerings** (Job1:1,5) for each of his sons, just in case they might have sinned. He was truly a good man. Life on this earth could not have been better!

Then disaster struck!

There was a conversation in heaven that changed everything for this family. The Lord was so pleased with Job, He was bragging on him! **There is none like him on the face of the earth.** (Job1:8) He told Satan. And Satan replied, Job is only faithful to you because you provide for him and protect him. Take away all he has and he will curse You! Test him, the Lord said, **Behold, all that he has is in your power; only do not lay a hand on his person** (Job1:12).

And so it began......A test....

One day a servant came running to the house telling them, all their oxen and donkeys had been stolen and all the herdsmen killed by Sabean raiders! He was the only one who escaped!

While he was telling Job what happened, another man came to the house! A terrible lightening storm came through and struck all seven hundred sheep and all the shepherds! He was the only one who escaped!

As this man was telling his story, a third man came with more bad news! Chaldeans came and stole all the camels and killed all the workers except him!

At that very moment a forth man came with the most devastating news of all! All of their children were together at their brother's house when a tornado came and destroyed the house and killed all of the brothers and sisters! And he was the only servant to escape.

Job did not scream and rant, blame and curse God. Instead **Job arose and tore his robe and shaved his head, and he fell to the ground and worshiped In all this Job did not sin or charge God with wrong** (Job 1:20,22) But....where was Mrs. Job?

Satan appeared before the Lord again and he wasn't convinced of Job's faithfulness. Job has not turned against you because you are still protecting his body! **And the Lord said Behold, he is in your hand, but spare his life.** (Job 2:6)

So Satan struck again! This timer with terrible, painful boils from the top of his head to the bottom of his feet.

What did Job do? He sat in ashes! People used to put ashes on their heads to show God they needed His mercy and help. Job didn't just put ashes on his head, he sat in ashes! He knew God could help him and he was begging for mercy!

Where was Mrs. Job in all this? Was she sharing his grief? Was she showing love and compassion? Did she turn to God and pray with her husband?

Satan struck Job again. He was really doing all he could to turn Job against God. This time, it was the worst thing he could possibly do to Job! His wife was all Job had left, and Satan used her!

Why don't you **Curse God and Die** (Job 2:9) Blame God and let Him kill you! Get it over! That was Mrs Job! Speaking to her husband! Has Satan finally won?

She was all Job had left. Did he do as she demanded? **No, you speak as one of the foolish women speak! Shall we indeed accept good from God, and shall we not accept adversity? In all this Job did not sin with his lips.** (Job 2:10)

We never hear of Mrs. Job again. Job, himself, after all these trials, and more to come, stayed faithful! And he was rewarded for his faithfulness!

Life is made of decisions. Everyday All day Little ones Big ones Unimportant ones and some that can forever change your life. Even your next life! God allows us to be tested. Ever since the beginning, humans were brought to life with a free will. And every day, Satan is watching for an opening. He uses everything he can, even people we love, to turn us against god. We are tested over and over. Job passed every test! Mrs Job failed every test!

1. She failed to be a helper for her husband. He needed her, they needed each other.
2. She failed the test of tribulation. She, herself, was burdened with sorrow and loss and refused to turn to God.
3. She failed the test of faith. She had lived with this man all those years; did she never share his faith in God? If so, where did it go?
4. She failed to see her opportunities. In every one of these trials, even in the midst of her sorrow, there were good, positive things she could have said and done.
5. She failed God! She turned her back on him. She blamed Him.

If she could send you a message now, what would it be?

Do not do what I did! In all circumstances, trust God!

Would she tell you to listen to the apostle Paul when he wrote to Timothy from a prison cell? **For this end we both labor and suffer reproach, because we trust in the living God.** (1Timothy 4:10)

FOOD FOR THOUGHT

1. It's easy to to be faithful and trust God when everything is going well and life is good. But what about when you loose your job and you have have kids to feed and bills to pay? Or when a pandemic hits your country?
   Acts 14:22 Romans 8:35-37 Romans 12:12

2. When we claim to be followers of God and His Son, but rather than trusting Him and doing His will, we really put our trust in ourselves? our Money? our Social standing? What then?
   Romans 2:8

3. What does Jesus say about trusting Him rather than ourselves?
   Matthew 6:19-34

SONG   SEEK YE FIRST

CHAPTER THREE

SARAI

Genesis 11:27-23:2

S arai was born in the land of Ur. Her father's name was Terah and she had three brothers, Abram, Nahor and Haran who died before our story begins. She also had a nephew, Lot, the son of Haran. And........she was married to her half brother, Abram.

Sarai and Abram had the same father but different mothers. (Genesis 20:12) It would be a long study to understand why or how intermarriage did not cause hereditary and genetic problems like it does today. But, it was a common thing then. There still were not that many people on the face of the earth.

Extended families all lived together and it could be a journey of weeks to go see a different family. Seven hundred years later when people had multiplied on the earth and were divided into a lot of different families, God gave His law to Moses and this was forbidden and has been ever since.

The people of Sarai's country were not God worshipers. They worshiped Nanna, the moon god among others. (Joshua 24:2) had Sarai and her family heard about the One True God? We aren't told.

When her father decided to move his family to Canaan, Nahor and his wife stayed in Ur. When the family got to Canaan, they settled in a place they named Haran. We don't know how long they were there, but we are told they were there long enough to greatly prosper. Their wealth, livestock and servants increased. This is where Sarai's father died. With Terah dead, Abram, as the oldest son, was now the head of the family.

Then one day, the Lord spoke to Abram! He told Abram to take his family and move **to a land I will show you. I will make you a great nation. I will bless you and make your name great** (Genesis12:1-2) Abram didn't question God! He packed up his family and went! No longer worshipers of Nanna.

And so it was, Sari's journey began. When they left Haran, Abram was seventy five years old and we are told in chapter seventeen, Sarai was ten years younger than her husband.

They came to a place called Bethel of Canaan and **there they built an altar and called on the name of the Lord,** (Genesis12:8) Wherever they went on their journey, they built an altar and worshiped God. Every time. As they continued their journey South, a famine hit the land, and they detoured into Egypt. When they arrived in Egypt, because Sarai was so beautiful, very exotic to the Egyptians, Abram instructed her to tell the people she was his sister not his wife! That way the people would not kill him to take her.

Again, this is a very strange thing to us, but evidently, it was alright with Sarai. But we will find out it wasn't alright with God!

It wasn't long before Pharaoh heard about the beautiful, exotic woman in the new band of nomads and had her brought to him. As a form of dowry, he gave Abram many sheep, oxen, donkeys, camels and servants. But before Pharaoh could have her made his wife, the Lord plagued the house of Pharaoh until he took her back to Abram and told him to take his wife and leave! Now! And Abram did. They headed South again, back to Bethel.

By this time, the family was very wealthy and he and Lot had such large increases in herd animals, the land could not support all of them in one place, and their herdsmen begin fighting with one another over the best land and water. So Abram decided it would be best if he and Lot separated households and went their own ways, so Lot agreed to move on. He picked the well watered plain of Jordan just outside the city of Sodom, and there he pitched his tents.

And Abram and Sarai lived in the land of Canaan. Again the Lord again spoke to Sarai's husband. **All the land which you see I give you and your descendants forever. Your descendants will be as the dust of the earth** (without number).(Genesis13:15,16) This is the second time God gave him that promise. Sarai and her husband moved again, to Hebron of Canaan, and built an altar and lived there.

About ten years pass, **and the word of the Lord came to Abram** (Genesis15:1) This is the first time we hear of that phrase.

SIDE NOTE: Who was "the Word" **The Word was with God in the beginning. The Word was with God and the Word was God. He was in the beginning with God.** (John 1:1,2) Then John tells us **The Word became flesh and dwelt among us.** (John 1:14)Jesus, the Christ...... Something to think about.

What did the Word tell Abram? You will have an heir and your descendents will be without number, **count the stars, if you are able to number them, so shall your descendents be.**

(Genesis15:1-5) This is the third time, God has made the same promise. But still, Abram and Sarai have no children. How is this promise to come true without children?

So Sarai comes up with a plan. (Genesis16:1-16) She talked Abram into giving her a child by a surrogate mother, her Egyptian maid, Hagar.

Abram agreed and trouble began. As soon as Hagar got pregnant, she began giving Sarai a hard time. Scripture tells us she hated her mistress! It got so bad, Sarai went to Abram and told him, this is all my fault, but something has to be done! Abram told her, Hagar belongs to you, do what you please. So Sarai made things so hard on Hagar, she ran away! The Lord met her along the way and told her to go back and submit to her mistress, and she did. When her son, Ishmael, was born,

Abram was eighty six years old and Sarai was seventy six. But this was not was God had planned for them!

Ten years later, her husband has another conversation with God. And again, He makes the same promise, but this time there is more! **No longer will you be called Abram, but your name will be called Abraham for I have made you a father of many nations. Kingdoms will come from you. I will establish My covenant between Me and you** (Genesis 17:5-7)

This was when circumcision was first introduced as an outward, physical sign of the covenant (agreement) made. God made conditions and Abraham agreed. (Kind of like signing a contract.) It was reintroduced when God spoke to Moses and stayed in effect until Christ brought the new covenant. (1Corinthians 11-23)

Then the Lord said **As for Sarai, your wife, you will not call her name Sarai, but Sarah shall be her name. I will bless her and give you a son by her; then I will bless her and she shall be the mother of many nations; kings of peoples shall be from her. And you shall call his name Isaac.** (Genesis 17:15-19)

Not long after that Sarah was in their tent when she overheard a conversation her husband was having with three men she didn't know. One of them said she was going to have a baby! Her! Sarah! She was ninety years old! And she laughed to herself. Somehow, one of the men knew she was laughing. How? She didn't laugh out loud. And He asked Abraham if anything was too hard for the Lord. Then he said when he would return the next year, she would have had her son.

During that following year a lot happened to Sarah and her family. Their tents are still just twenty six miles from Hebron. The city, Sodom, where Lot had finally gone to live, was destroyed by God because of its wickedness. (Genesis 19)

After that, she and Abraham move to Gerar. This is where they get in trouble again for telling the same "half truth". King Abimelach of Gerar is stricken by the beauty of Sarah and takes her for his wife! She is ninety years old, expecting and still irresistibly beautiful! Again,

God intervenes and Sarah is released unharmed. (Genesis 20) Peace was restored and they remain in Gerar.

Finally, after twenty five years of waiting, Sarah had her son, Isaac. (Genesis 21:2-3) And Hagar gave her so much grief that Abraham stepped in and sent her and her son away.

Abraham and King Abimelach have another run-in. This time over water wells and they finally make a truce. And that is when Abraham finally gave their home a name, Beersheba (Genesis 21:31) This is where we first hear of the Philistines, and they were a thorn in the flesh of God's people from then on!

One day Sarah's husband and her son went up on the mountain to offer a sacrifice to the Lord. According to Josephus, a first century historian, Isaac was twenty five years old at the time. When they came back, they had an unbelievable story to tell Sarah! Abraham almost killed her son! (Genesis 22) But it was only a test. The Lord was testing Abraham's faith, and Abraham passed the test! He was willing to sacrifice his only son, but only because he knew God would raise him up again! (Hebrews 11:17-19)

Twelve years later, Sarah died. She was and hundred and twenty years old. Abraham bought some land with a cave on it and there he buried Sarah. (Genesis 23:1-2, 19-20)

And the promises God made Sarah came true even though she did not live to see it happen. She did not live to see her son, Isaac married. She did not live to see Isaac's twelve grandsons who became the "Children of Israel" until they became known as the "Nation of Israel", who grew to over three million people! And then increased even more and produced kings; Saul, David and eventually....Jesus, Himself! What a family she started.

The last time we hear about Sarah, the writer of Hebrews lists her name in the "Hall of Faith"

By faith Sarah herself also received strength to conceive seed and she bore a child when she was past the age, because she judged Him faithful who had promised. (Hebrews 11:11)

What would Sarah's message be?

Nothing is too hard for the Lord! Believe. Be patient. Wait for Him. He will do what He promised, in His time.

For My thoughts are not your thoughts,
Nor are your ways My ways, says the Lord.
For as the heavens are higher than the earth, so are My ways higher than your ways, and My thoughts than your thoughts. (Isaiah 55:8-9)

FOOD FOR THOUGHT

1. Do you believe in all of God's promises?

2. Have you given up on God keeping His promises?
    2Peter 3:8-9   Matthew 19:26
    Matthew 19:26

3. Are there promises in the Bible that apply to you?
    Isiah 43:13   Isiah 55:8   John 3:16
    Jeremiah 29:12-13   2 Corinthians 12:9-10
    1John 1:9   Matthew 11:28-29   Psalm 32:8
    John 14:27   Isiah41:10

Can you find more? There are about 160 promises in the Bible

SONG   **STANDING ON THE PROMISES**

CHAPTER FOUR

LOT'S WIFE

Genesis 18 & 19

She and her family lived in the city of Sodom. It was really two cities grown together, Sodom and Gomorrah; we would call them "sister cities". Studies have been made about the population of these two cities and the area around them. The guess is probably between fifty and a hundred thousand. Some say more.

She was married to a very wealthy business man and "rancher". He was also member of what we might call a city council. These men sat by the city gate to conduct business and settle disputes between citizens.

She had sons and daughters and sons-in-law and two younger daughters still at home.

Everything sounds good, except Sodom and Gomorrah was the most wicked city in the world! And what was the cause of all that wickedness? The word sodomy comes from the word Sodom. And sodomy is sex between two men, or two women, or a man or woman with an animal! Gomorrah mean vice and corruption! Everything was lawful and accepted. And no one there objected to this kind of living!

These things have been against God's law since the beginning! Leviticus 18:22-23 Romans 1:26-38

God, Himself called called these things an abomination and a perversion!

One day the Lord came to visit Lot's uncle Abraham, as He often did. This time He told Abraham, because of the wickedness of the people, He was going to destroy the city where his nephew and his family lived.

Abraham pleaded with the Lord **Would you also destroy the righteous with the wicked?** If you find fifty good people would you save the city? And God replied Yes. Abraham thought about how wicked the place was and asked God if he would save the city for just forty five righteous. And again God agreed. Abraham thought again and asked God to save the city for forty good people, then again and again until he asked God to save the city if only ten righteous souls could be found! And God said I will not destroy it for the sake of ten. Just ten good people out of a hundred thousand!!! Surly there were ten! (Genesis 18:16-33)

God sent two angels who looked like men, to Sodom to talk to Lot. They were immediately attacked by the men of that city who wanted to abuse them with their wickedness. The angels struck the men blind and told Lot, if you have any family in the city go get them, **Whomever you have in this city-- take them out of this place! For we will destroy this place** (Genesis 19:12-13)

Just ten good people will save the city! But when Lot went to his sons-in-law and told them what was going to happen, they laughed at him! Morning came and still Lot had not left the city. Again the angels told him to take his wife and the two daughters who still lived at home and get out of this city! What was Lot's wife thinking in all of this? Those men were going to destroy her children, her home and everything they owned and all their friends. Finally the angels took them by their hands and led them out of the city! When they were out of the city the angel said **Escape for your life! Do not look back behind you, nor stay anywhere in the plain. Escape to the mountains.** (Genesis19: 12-17)

And again Lot protested! Can you believe it? Let us go to a nearby little city, not the wilderness; we may come to harm there. This man had no faith in God or His protection or His provision at all!!

The angel agreed. If that is what you want, but hurry. Lot, his wife and two daughters walked all that day and night. They reached the city of Zoar just at daybreak. And that was the very instant fire came from heaven and destroyed their home town! And they had escaped! The Lord saw to it, in spite of themselves! Why did the Lord offer him a way of escape? Make him escape? God gave Lot and his family a second chance because **God remembered Abraham.** (Genesis19:2) He remembered how Abraham had begged Him to give Lot a chance to start over!

They escaped! Made it to safety! What was it the angel had told them not to do?

But Lot's wife looked back! And was instantly turned into a pillar of salt! (Genesis19:26)

We know Lot knew about God. He lived with his uncle for years. He helped him build altars and worship God. Lot knew his uncle and the Lord had conversations over the years. Did Lot ever tell his wife and children about those times?

If Lots wife could send us a message, what would she say to us?

The Lord gave me a second chance! He gave me an opportunity to turn my life around and start over and I refused! Abraham was imploring the Lord on my behalf! And I didn't care.

Or do you despise the riches of His goodness, forbearance, and longsuffering, not knowing that the goodness of God leads to repentance? (Rom 2:4)

FOOD FOR THOUGHT

1. Has God given you a second chance? A third chance?
   Reflect   Remember   Thank Him

       John 5:14   John 8:11   Romans 1:21-22
       Romans 3: 23-25   2Peter 3:9   1 John 1:9-10

2. Have you prayed that God would use you to turn someone from bad choices?
       Acts 16:25   1Peter 3:1   Matthew 5:14-16

3. Have you prayed that God would give someone else time to make a change and turn themselves over to Him?
       Ephesians 6:18   1Timothy 2:1   Colossians 1:9
       Matthew 5:44

SONG   **FATHER FORGIVE US**

CHAPTER 5

REBEKAH

Genesis 24-28:5

Rebekah grew up in the city of Nahor. Her father was Bethuel. Her grandfather, Nahor had a brother named Abraham who left home years ago, before she was born.

One day she went to the well for water and there was a man there she had never seen before and he said he was a servant of her great uncle Abraham! She invited him to her brother's house where he then gave them the message from Abraham.

Abraham had told his servant to go to Nahor and the Lord would would give him a sign to know which young woman He would choose to become the wife of Abraham's son, Isaac. The Lord's choice turned out to be Rebekah, if she and her family were willing. Abraham had sent several men with his servant and they had brought gifts of gold and silver jewelry and fine clothing for Rebekah and precious things for her brother, Laban and her mother. (Genesis 24:53) When Rebekah was asked if she was willing, her answer was yes. So her family packed Rebekah and her maids and sent them to Abraham.

Then Isaac brought her into his mother Sarah's tent; and he took Rebekah and she became his wife and he loved her. So Isaac was comforted after his mother's death. (Genesis 24:67) We are never told she loved him. She had married into a wealthy family and she had the best of everything, but she could not not have children. After twenty years of waiting, Isaac finally pleaded with the Lord and she conceived, but something wasn't right. There was too much constant movement in her womb. So she asked the Lord **If all is well, why am I this way? And the Lord said to her:**

> **Two nations are in your womb,**
> **Two peoples shall be separated from your body;**
> **One people shall be stronger than the other,**
> **And the older shall serve the younger.**
>
> Genesis 25: 22-23)

Twins!! The first twins ever recorded! And when they were born, they were nothing alike. Not in looks, attitude, interests, nothing! Esau was always a rugged outdoors man and Jacob was a mild mannered, quiet man. And then....one of the greatest mistake any parent can make and Jacob and Rebekah both made it! Issac made no secret of the fact he loved Esau and Rebekah openly preferred Jacob. Because of this, the two boys grew to be men who who were enemies!

One day Esau came in from the field, tired and hungry. What he had been doing, how far away this field was, how tired and hungry he was, we are not told. But he was willing to sell his birthright to his younger brother for a meal! **Esau ate and drank arose and went his way. Thus Esau despised** (turned his back on, got rid of) **his birthright.** (Genesis 25:29-34). He didn't want it! He saw a chance to get rid of it and sold it for a meal!

Did he just not want the responsibility? All the work of ownership?

What was a birthright? When Isaac would die, all of his material holding; money, herds, land, businesses, workers, servants, everything would be divided between his sons, with the oldest receiving the larger share and becoming the head of the family. Now, Jacob, the younger son, would get everything!

A famine came and the Lord spoke to Issac and told him to move on and he did. And what happened next is going to sound so familiar!

Isaac moved everything and everybody to the land of Gerar in the land of the Philistines. Rebekah was so beautiful and exotic looking the men of Gerar begin noticing her and Isaac told her to pass herself as his sister, not his wife! This time it was not even a half truth, it was a lie! It wasn't long before everyone had heard about the man and his beautiful sister!

And guess who was still king? Abimelech! One day, the king saw Isaac and Rebekah together and he knew! The king immediately went to Isaac and asked, what would have happened if one of my people had taken her to be his wife? So to protect his own people, King Abimelech put out a decree saying any man who touches Issac or Rebekah will be put to death!

So they lived there in peace until the Philistines noticed how Isaac's crops produced a hundredfold that year: his flocks and herds increased as had the number of servants. The Philistines were in such an uproar, the king finally told Isaac to move on! Isaac and his large holdings had become a threat to the king! He had become wealthier than the king and the Philistines envied him. (Genesis 26:12-16)

So Isaac and Rebekah moved on and everywhere they went, the Philistines came after them and stopped up the water wells so there was no water for them or their herds and flocks.

Finally they came to Beersheba and the Lord appeared to Isaac that very night. **I am the God of your father Abraham; do not fear for I am with you. I will bless you and multiply your descendants for my servant, Abraham's sake.** (Genesis 26:24)

Again, God is helping a man, not because he is faithful, but because He made a promise to Abraham, and Isaac is the one to receive and carry out part of that promise. This is the first time we read of Isaac building an altar and worshiping God. Then they pitched their tents, dug a well and made their home. It wasn't long before Abimelech showed up. The king was convinced that the Lord was with Isaac and wanted to make a covenant of peace. The family stayed put and the place Abraham first named Beersheba, would one day become a city.

When Rebekah's first born son was twenty, he took not just one wife, but two. They were of the Hitite nation! Godless, idol worshiping people, and they were a constant worry to Isaac and Rebekah.

Years go by and her husband's wealth was growing but other things aren't so good. Her sons didn't get along, her two daughters-in-law were a constant problem and her husband had slowly gone blind.

Isaac was more than a hundred years old, maybe as old as a hundred and twenty, and he didn't know how much longer he would live so he called for his oldest son Esau, to prepare a special meal and be ready to receive his father's blessing.

Rebekah overheard the conversation and went to Jacob and convinced him to deceive his father in order to receive the blessing. Jacob was to disguise himself as Esau, take the special meal his mother would prepare and go to his father and receive the blessing.

Jacob already had his brother's birthright, his inheritance of all that his father owned. A blessing was different. This was a foretelling of what the future held for the son. It was divinely inspired; Only God knew what was going to be said.

Now remember, God had spoken to Rebekah fifty years earlier when she was pregnant with her boys. She remembered the Lord's plan; her sons would become two nations and the older would serve the younger. She had to make sure Jacob received the blessing, and her plan worked!

Jacob received the blessing; it confirmed what God had told Rebekah years ago. God would provide for and protect Jacob and make him a nation so powerful, that other nations, including the nation his brother would build, would serve him and his descendants. (Genesis 27:27-29)

As soon as Jacob left the room, Esau came in. When he found out what had happened, he was angry and hurt. He begged his father to bless him also. Again, only God knows the reasons for future events and the future for Esau was not what Esau wanted.

Esau was told his descendants would serve his brother's descendants until they would finally rebel and break free. (Genesis 27:39-40)

All of these predictions of the future came true.

The nation of Judah were the descendants of Jacob's son, Judah. (Genesis 29:35) through whom came Jesus, the Christ.

Esau became the father of the nation known as the Edomites (Genesis 36:1,43)

About a thousand years later, **Edom revolted against Judah and made a king over themselves. Thus, Edom has been in revolt against Judah's authority until this day,** (2Kings 8:20,22)

When Esau heard the blessing, he hated his brother and made a vow; I will wait until my father dies and then I will kill him!

When Rachel heard about what Esau had said, she told Jacob to leave and go to her brother, Laban in Haran. Stay there a few days until your brother calms down and I will send for you. Then she went to her husband. Do something! My life is so bad, if I loose Jacob, what will I have left? So Isaac told Jacob to leave Beersheba and go to Haran, to his mother's people and get a wife.

Jacob left Beersheba and Rachel never saw her son again.

Did Rebekah ever hear from him or about him? Did she know she had twelve grandsons by him? Did she know God had spoken to her son, just like God had spoken to his father and to her? Did she know God changed her son's name to Israel?

The last we hear of her, Paul wrote to the church in Rome concerning God's sovereignty and His plans to bring salvation through His Son. He wrote about Rebekah and what God told her: **The older shall serve the younger.**(Romans 9:12)

What would Rebekah's message be?

Believe what God tells you! It will happen! Today, tomorrow, a thousand years from now; it will happen!

In hope of eternal life which God, who cannot lie, promised before time began. (Titus 1:2)

FOOD FOR THOUGHT

1. Rebekah didn't live long enough to see God's promise to her come true. God and His Son made a lot of promises through the years, Here are just a few.

Isiah 41:10	Has God kept this one?
John 16:33	Is God keeping this one?
Matthew 11:28-29	Is Jesus keeping this one?
Mark 16:16	Does Jesus keep this one?
Matthew 6:31-33	Does Jesus keep this one?
John 3:16-18	Do you think this one will come true?

2. Sometimes God used people, like Rebekah to make His plan happen and to begin with, they didn't know or understand, so they didn't cooperate with Him until He did something to get their attention! Sometimes, after these people could see what God was doing and the results of His actions, they became believers! Are there other examples in the bible of God using and changing imperfect people for His cause?

   What about the twelve men Jesus chose to be his apostles? Did they change over night?

3. Do we always understand why, when or how the Lord does things? Isaiah 55:8-9 2Peter 3:8-9

SONG **SWEET ARE THE PROMISES**

CHAPTER SIX

RACHEL

Genesis 29-35

Her story is the beginning of the Israelite Nation. When we first meet Rachel, she is a shepherdess for her father, Laban and she came to the well to water her flocks. There was a man there who helped her water her flocks and he told her, his mother, Rebekah was her father's sister.

It was love at first sight! We are told several times in their story, of how much he loved her, but we are never told she loved him. Not one time!

Her father came to meet her and greeted Jacob. When Laban found out who he was, he took Jacob home with him and he stayed a month. Then Laban said Jacob could not continue to work for nothing, and asked him what he thought a fair wage would be and Jacob made him a proposition: **I will serve you seven years for Rachel your younger daughter** (Genesis 29:18) Laban agreed.

At the end of the seven years, Laban proved himself to be a liar and deceiver. At the appointed time, a big banquet was held, following by the wedding. As was the custom, the bride was covered with veils and after an evening of eating and drinking, Jacob had a rude awakening ! His new bride was not Rachel, but her older sister, Leah! (Genesis29:25)

When he confronted Laban, Laban said, In our country, the oldest daughter must be married first. Nobody explained this to Jacob seven years earlier! Leah knew! Rachel knew! For seven years Rachel deceived him! They saw each other every day. Did Jacob make plans with her, talk about their future? What about when the plans were made for the wedding day? The banquet, the wedding garments?

Why didn't he run for his life? But Jacob was so in love with Rachel, he accepted the solution Laban offered. Give Leah her wedding week and then I will give you Rachel and you will work for me seven more years. (Genesis29:26-27)

Now Jacob has two wives, sisters, and his troubles have just begun! Time goes by and Leah gave birth to four sons and Rachel has no children.

The belief was, among God's children as well as pagans, that if a woman was barren, it was a punishment from God or one of the false gods. Supposedly, there was sin in the woman's life. So, the other side of this belief is; the more children a woman has, the more she is favored by God, or which ever god she worships. So it was, a woman was shamed if she had no children and she was rewarded if she did.

Now we see another side of Rachel. Jealousy and anger. It sounds like she is blaming Jacob! She is determined to have children! So she tells Jacob to give her children by a surrogate mother, her maid Bilhah.

(Who does this remind you of? Sarah and Hagar. How well did that turn out? The descendants of those two boys are still at war, 2000 years later!)

When Rachel's maid gave birth to a second son, we see another side of Rachel! Now she is gloating! Now I have won; I am truly number one wife! But the war isn't over yet!

Leah gave her maid to her husband as a surrogate for her. Before this competition is over, there are eleven sons, with one more to come later and several daughters. We only know the name of one, Diana, but Genesis 37:35 tells us there were more.

Rachel and Leah were never at peace with each other. Leah accused her of taking her husband away from her, but she knew all along, Jacob loved Rachel. Leah was the first wife but never the "live-in" wife. But now, she has given birth to six sons and her maid has had two and she is sure her husband would live with her. It never happened! Do we read she wanted to be in his tent because she loved him? No! She just wanted to be number one. Were either one of these women happy?

God finally remembered Rachel and she had a son and named him Joseph. (Genesis 30:22-23)

At the end of the second seven year period of servitude, Jacob tells Laban, he wants to go home and begin building his own live and fortune. But, Laban's wealth has increased and his flocks have increased under Jacob's care, so Laban again begs him to stay and this time, Jacob makes the offer.

Don't pay me anything. I will take care of all your flocks and you will receive all the profits. But give me a place of my own and all the speckled and spotted sheep will belong to me, and all the profits I make from from those sheep will me mine. Laban agreed. Everyone knew speckled and spotted sheep were inferior, they were weaker and did not reproduce like the pure bred white animals.

With God's help, Jacob's flocks became larger, stronger and multiplied greatly. He bought servants and hired workers and then bought camels and donkeys and built wealth for his family.

Meanwhile, Laban's purebred flocks have diminished! They have become weaker and less in numbers. Laban's sons were not happy!

Then the Lord told Jacob, now is the time to go. **Return to the land of your father and your kindred, and I will be with you.** (Genesis 31:3)

Jacob was ready! When he told his wives, **you know I have served your father with all my might. Yet your father had deceived me and changed my wages ten times but God did not allow him to hurt me** (Genesis 31:6-7) Twenty years is enough! I am ready to go home!

Rachel and her sister answered him: We don't have any choice! Do we have an inheritance here? Our **father has sold us and also** completely consumed our money. **For all these riches which God has taken from our father are really ours and our children's;** (not yours) **now then whatever God has said to you, do it.** (Genesis 31:15-16) Do you hear any love from Rachel? Rachel will go with him, not because she loves him, but he has all her father's money, and it really is hers!

When Laban left on a business trip, Jacob packed up his family and all that belonged to him and left for home. A week later, Laban caught up with him and was he MAD! Not only did Jacob steal his family away from him but some one stole his gods! The camp was searched, but the idols were not found. Rachel had hidden them! She has proven herself to be a liar, a deceiver and now a thief! (Genesis 31:19-41)

For twenty years she has watched her husband worship God, listen to God, obey and be blessed by God! And still she clings to her idols! She is her father's daughter in every way!

Further on in their journey, the daughter, Dinah, gets involved with a man named Shechem, a prince of the Hivite people. Again, these people were not God worshipers. Shechem's father is willing to make a treaty with these nomads in order for his son to have what he wants. But before Jacob could make an answer, his sons stepped in with a prepared, deceitful plan. (Genesis 34:13) Jacob's sons said, if all of the males in your city will become circumcised then we can make a treaty with you. They agreed and all the males were circumcised. Three days later, when everyone of them were in bed in pain, the sons of Isaac struck! They entered the city and killed Shechem and his father and every man in the city! They took all their animals, their wealth, took all the women and children captive and robbed all the houses.

When Jacob found out what they had done, he told them, we will all be killed for this! The other cities will come after us and we are too few to fight them off! And his sons answered: what else could we have done? They were their mother's sons! Liars and deceivers and now murderers!

God instructed Jacob to leave and go to Bethel. Jacob told his family to get rid of all the false gods they had and all the gold earrings they were wearing, which were a symbol of belonging to these false gods.

And Jacob hid them under a great tree and took his family away from there and went to Bethel. And God saw to it that the other cities didn't come after them.

When they reached Bethel, Jacob built an altar and Again God appeared to Jacob and said to him, **You name is Jacob; your name shall not be called Jacob anymore, but Israel shall be your name.** (Genesis 35:10) And God gave the same promise to Israel He had given to Abraham. Nations will come from you and kings from your seed. And all the land of Canaan will one day belong to your offspring.

They continued on their way and Rachel went into hard labor and gave birth to her second son, Benjamin, but she died as the result. **So Rachel died and was buried on the way to Ephrath, (that is Bethleham).** (Genesis 35:19)

Now there are twelve sons of Israel. But God will have His hands full with these twelve boys and their offspring!

When Rachel's son, Joseph was just seventeen, his brothers sold him to slave traders! And he was taken into Egypt and sold as a slave to the Egyptians!

God makes these boys into a nation but they are their mother's sons. They just could not leave the foreign gods behind! (Judges 2:11-15) It was just easier for them to believe in something they could see and touch. Eventually, because of their love of false gods the Lord had their nation destroyed!!

This is the end of Rachel's story but then several hundred years later, when the Israelite Nation was taken captive, the prophet, Jeremiah wrote: **Thus says the Lord: A voice was heard in Ramah, Lamentation and bitter weeping. Rachel weeping for her children, Refusing to be comforted for her children, Because they are no more.** (Jeremiah 31:15)

What would Rachel's message be? I think she has two messages for us.

First, the things we say and do have consequences that affect the lives of our children and grandchildren.

Do not be deceived, God is not mocked; for whatever a man sows, that he will also reap. (Galatians 6:7)

Second, Do not worship or bow down to any god or idol except the Lord God.

"I am the way, the truth and the life. No one comes to the Father except by Me." (John 14:6)

FOOD FOR THOUGHT

1. What Rachel said and did had consequences. What were they?

2. What does the Bible say about idols?
    Exodus 20:4-5, 34:13-16 2   Kings 17:9-23   Hosea 4:12-19
    Acts 17:29   Romans 1:22-25   1 Corinthians 10:14, 19-21

3. How can we live lives that will have good consequences for generations to come?
    Proverbs 31:10-31   Galatians 5:22-26

    compare these two parents: 1Kings 15:11 and 1Kings 11:26

4. What will be the consequences of your life? Is it too late to change direction?

    Acts 8:22   Matthew 3:8   2Corinthians 7:9-10

SONG   **LIVING FOR JESUS**

CHAPTER SEVEN

PUAH AND SHIPHRAH

Exodus 1: 7-20

Y ou can not tell the story of Puah without telling the story of Shiphrah. They are one and the same.

Their story begins with the twelve sons of Jacob, who God had renamed Israel. It was one of Jacobs' sons, Joseph, who had been sold as a slave to the Egyptians forty years earlier.

The Egyptian Pharaoh held Joseph in such high respect and honor he had promoted him to second in command over all Egypt.

Then forty years later, Joseph's family, a total of seventy persons, had arrived in Egypt to escape a famine in their homeland. Pharaoh invited the family to stay, He gave them the best land in Egypt for their flocks and offered them employment as chief herdsmen for his livestock. And they were all living there in a free and peaceful relationship.(Genesis 47:6)

As the years went by, The **children of Israel had been fruitful and increased abundantly, multiplied and grew exceedingly mighty;** and now, years later, **the land was full of them!** (Exodus 1:7)

Now, generations later. a new Pharoah, who never heard of Joseph was in power and he was worried about these people; they were exceedingly strong, healthy men! What if they decided to join with Pharaoh's enemies and over run the Egyptians! Things changed! Now Israel's family were no longer a free people, some of which were employees of Pharaoh; now they were made slaves!

The hard work of slavery only made the people stronger, so Pharaoh increased their work load. But the harder he worked them, the stronger they became and they multiplied in number until the Egyptians were afraid of them.

So the Egyptians made them work harder; increased their work load and tried to work them to death! But they continued to multiply and grow stronger!

So Pharaoh came up with a plan to reduce the numbers of the Hebrews. He called the midwives of Israel in to talk to them and this is where we meet Puah and Shiprah. They were part of the Israelite family and they the were midwives to their women.

He gave a command to Puah and Shiprah, when you serve the Hebrew women as midwives, and you are helping deliver a baby boy, kill him at birth! But if the baby is a daughter, she may live.

But Puah and Shiphrah **feared God and did not do as the king of Egypt commanded them, but saved the male children alive.** (Exodus 1:17)

Why did these women fear God? They knew the history of their people! They knew the power God had to destroy His enemies and the power He had to preserve His people! They saw how God had given their people strong, healthy, enduring bodies! God had made their people a mighty people in spite of everything Pharaoh had done to them! That is why they feared God! No one, not even Pharoah was more powerful than God!

When Pharaoh heard what they were doing, he called them in again. What have you done? What have you disobeyed a direct command of mine? The women told him, The Hebrew women are not like Egyptian women. Our women are very strong and healthy. They have their babies before we can get to them!

The result?

God took care of the midwives, **and the people multiplied and grew very mighty.** (Exodus 1: 20)

That is all we hear of Puah and Shiphrah, only seven verses out of the whole Bible, but what an example they leave us! They disobeyed a direct command of Pharaoh! What courage they showed! What faith they displayed!

If these two women could send us a message, what would it be?

Wherever you live, whatever your circumstances, what ever government you live under, fear God rather than man! Love God for His mercy, His grace. Trust Him for His provision and His protection, and fear Him for his great power and obey Him!

We ought to obey God rather than man.

(Acts 5:29)

FOOD FOR THOUGHT

1. Do you love God? fear Him? obey Him?
    Deuteronomy 6:5   Matthew10:28   Joshua 24:24

2. If the people in our community should make it difficult for us to live
    as Christians, or the law of our land should outlaw Christianity....
    Who do you fear more? God or man? Who do you want to please
    more? Who do you trust more? God or man?

    Psalm 27:1   Matthew 10:28   Hebrews 13:6

    Galatians 1:10

3. Do we have the courage to stand up for God and be counted?

    Deuteronomy 31: 6   Daniel 3:16-18   1Peter 4:12-16

SONG   **TRUST AND OBEY**

CHAPTER EIGHT

JOCHEBED

Exodus 1 & 2 Exodus 6:20

The Children of Israel have now been slaves in Egypt for four hundred years. They have multiplied and become stronger and mightier. And now there are more than three million of them! Enter Jochebed and her family! Jochebed and her husband were descendants of the family of Levi, the third born of Jacob (Israel). She and her husband, Amran, their daughter, Miriam and son, Aaron were slaves of Egypt, (Exodus 6:20) and she was expecting another child

The Pharaoh had done all he could to work the Hebrews to death, but they had only increased in strength and number, so he came up with another way to weaken them and still have slaves to do his work. He spoke to the Hebrew midwives and told them, **When you do the duties of a midwife for the Hebrew women, and see them on the birthstools, if it is a son, then you shall kill him; but if it is a daughter, then she shall live.** (Exodus 1:16) This was the same solution a pharaoh years ago had tried to enforce.

And again, the midwives told him, by the time they were called, the babies had already been born and there was nothing they could do.

So.....he came up with another plan. He didn't need the help of the midwives, He told his own people, every time the Hebrew women have a son, **every son that is born you shall cast into the river, and every daughter you shall save alive.** (Exodus 1:22) The Nile river was full of crocodiles!

You know Jochebed was scared to death when her baby turned out to be a boy! A beautiful, special boy. But rather than obey Pharaoh, her faith in the Lord God of Israel caused her to hide her baby. For three months she hid him, but when she could no longer keep him a secret, she put him in a basket and set him afloat on the Nile river. A river full of crocodiles! But.......she knew he was in God's hands.

Her baby was rescued by the daughter of Pharaoh, who asked Jochebed to raise him until he was weaned, somewhere between ages three and five. How much can you teach a baby about God? Will he remember any thing? If you tell him over and over that God loves him? Will he remember? Will he remember any of the songs, any of the words you sing or pray? Then her baby was taken to the house of Pharaoh and raised as his grandson. Pharaoh's daughter named the baby Moses. (Exodus2:10)

I can not imagine what Jochebed was feeling through all this. Her beautiful little boy would be raised as the son of Pharaoh's daughter. He would become the master of his own people! An Egyptian. But, that was not God's plan.

In Acts 7, Stephen was reviewing the history of the Jewish nation when he was on trial before the Jewish Council. When he began talking about the life of Moses, he said: **When Moses was was forty years old, it came into his heart to visit his brethren, the children of Israel. And seeing one of them suffer wrong, he defended him and avenged him.........For he supposed that his brethren would have understood that God would deliver them by his hand, but they did not understand.** (Acts7:20-25) Somehow God let Moses knew he would be the deliverer, but Moses got ahead of God and......... tragedy struck! Moses killed an Egyptian taskmaster and he thought the Israelites would have understood he was trying to help them, but they didn't. They were afraid of him and turned on him!

When Pharaoh heard about it, he wanted Moses killed, so Moses, at forty years old, ran for his life.

Did Jochebed hear from him again? Was she still living forty years later, when God sent her son back to Egypt to speak with Pharaoh? Would she know her son would be the one God would choose to rescue her people and bring them out of slavery? Was she among those delivered?

Jochebed shows up in scripture one more time. Fourteen hundred and fifty years later, the writer of Hebrews includes her and her husband in the famous list of "Heroes of Faith".

By faith Moses, when he was three months old was hidden by his parents, because they saw he was a beautiful child and they were not afraid of the kings command. (Hebrews 11:23)

We do not hear any more about Jochebed, but we do know her faith, produced the man to whom the One True God spoke! They spoke together as friends, all through Moses's later life. Her son was the one to whom God would deliver the Ten Commandments and the laws which would direct her people until Christ would bring the last testament.

What would Jochebed's message be to us?

No matter the circumstances, call on your faith! It will help you make right decisions and give you peace to endure all trials, disappointments, fears and unrest.

Therefore, having been justified by faith, we have peace with God through our Lord, Jesus Christ. (Romans 5:1)

FOOD FOR THOUGHT

1. What did Jochebed's faith help her do?

2. What is faith?
   Hebrew 11:1

3. Where does faith come from?
   John 20:30-31   Romans 10:17   Hebrews 12:2
                        1John 5:13

4. What does faith help us do?
   James chapters 2,3,4

SONG   **FAITH IS THE VICTORY**

CHAPTER NINE

MIRIAM

Exodus 2:1-10   Exodus 15:19-21
Numbers 12 and 20:1

When we first see Miriam she was a little girl who had a brother, three years old and a new baby brother. She and her parents and her family for generations had been slaves in Egypt. She was the litle girl who's mother put her baby brother in a basket and put him afloat in the crocodile infested Nile River! **And his sister stood afar off, to know what would be done to him.** (Exodus 2:4)

Her brother was rescued and raised by Pharaoh's daughter who named him Moses.

The Egyptians had lots of gods, but her people, the Israelites, had only one; The Creator, God, The God of promises to her ancestors. But it seemed to some of her people, that their God had forgotten about them! Their lives had become so hard!

Time went by and her brother, Moses was forty years old when he killed an Egyptian. Then he had to leave the country because Pharaoh was going to take Moses's life! Miriam's brother was gone!

Forty more years go by and her other brother, Aaron went to find Moses. When Aaron came home, he had Moses with him! And they had an incredible story!

God, Himself had talked to the two brothers and told them, they were to go back and talk to Pharaoh! Moses was to ask Pharaoh to release their people! After four hundred and thirty years! Freedom!

The first visit with Pharaoh did not go well. He refused to let his slaves go. Miriam watched as the God of Israel rained down a terrible plague on Egypt. All the water in Egypt turned to blood! And the Egyptian god of the Nile, Hapi was proven helpless! And Pharaoh still refused to let the people go.

Again Miriam watched as God sent seven more terrible plagues, each worse than the others. And each one defeated another god of Egypt! And still Pharaoh refused to let the people go!

And then God sent a terrible darkness, one that could be felt! It lasted three days and nights! Where was Ra, the Egyptian sun god then?

The God of Israel proved He was more powerful than all the gods of Egypt! And still Pharaoh refused!

Then her brother told the people, God was going to send one more plague and this time the Israelites had instructions to follow to protect themselves from the wrath of God that would strike all Egypt!

Then Moses told them the oddest thing! Each household was to kill a lamb at the appointed hour, and put blood of the lamb on the outside of the two doorposts and lintel of their house! Then they were to prepare a special meal; prepare the lamb an in a special way and particular foods to go with it.

Get packed up, dressed and ready to leave, but.... once everything is prepared and your meal eaten, do not go out of your door until morning! (Exodus 12:1-28) Miriam and her family and all the Israelites went to their homes and followed his instructions.

Her family had followed all the instructions. They killed a lamb, put blood on the outside of their doorposts, ate their meal, packed up and cleaned everything up, then they closed their door and locked it for the night.

At midnight Miriam heard the sound of wailing! It got louder and louder! It came from their Egyptian neighbors! All of Egypt; every unprotected house was in mourning! Every person who was a first born in their family died that same hour! (Are you the oldest sibling in your family?) Every mother lost her oldest child, no matter how old that child was! Even the house of Pharaoh!

Open your Bible and read Exodus 121:29-36

Pharaoh finally had enough! Leave! All of you! Take anything, everything you want and get out!!!! And they did! And the Egyptians gave them gold, silver, clothing, supplies, everything they could carry, and helped them leave!

Miriam and the Israelites walked of out Egypt. Six hundred thousand men plus women, children and older men; about three million people! Even some Egyptians were convinced of the power of their God and went with them!

Several days after they left, Pharaoh changed his mind! How stupid can one man be?!? He sent his army after them and when the Israelites saw them coming in the distance, they panicked! They were caught between the army of Pharaoh and the Red Sea! No way out! They were all going to die! Better off when they were Pharaoh's slaves! Doubting God! Blaming Moses!

Miriam watched as God caused a strong wind to roll back the waters of the Red Sea and dry out the sea bed so they could walk across on dry land! And the army kept coming!

When the last of the Israelites and their herds and flocks climbed on shore, Miriam and all the people watched as their God caused the water to roll back into place and drown all the Egyptians! Men, chariots, weapons, horses; all gone, not one survived! **Not so much as one of them remained**.(Exodus 14:28

At some point, God had made Miriam a prophetess and when Moses and the children of Israel broke into a song of celebration and thanksgiving Miriam sang an answering chorus!

"Sing to the Lord,
For He has triumphed gloriously!
The horse and its rider
He has thrown into the sea!"

(Exodus 15:21)

And so the journey to Canaan began, they were finally going to the land long ago promised to Abraham (Genesis 12:14-15) And God used Moses to guide and instruct His people along their journey.

Somewhere along the way, Aaron and Miriam began resenting their brother, envying him. The first thing they began complaining about was Moses wife!(Numbers 12:1) He had married this woman forty years ago! When he first left Egypt, when Pharaoh wanted to kill him for killing the Egyptian taskmaster. She had come to be with him not long after their journey to Canaan began. (Exodus 18:1-5)

And somehow Aaron and Miriam reasoned, Moses' marriage should have been enough reason for God to take the leadership role away from Moses and give it to them.

The second thing they resented was, they did not like Moses being God's number one spokesperson! **Has the Lord indeed spoken only through Moses? Has He not spoken through us also?**(Numbers12:2) God had spoken to both Aaron and Miriam, for they were both prophets. We are never told any of the things God told her to say, but, she wanted to be more than just a prophetess, she wanted to be the leader!

Sometimes, there is no connecting the dots! What did the marriage of Moses have to do with his leading the Israelites? They just wanted to pull Moses down! They wanted to be in charge! Jealousy, Envy!

God overheard their conversation and **suddenly the Lord said to Moses, Aaron and Miriam "Come out, you three to the tabernacle of meetings!"** Then He appeared as a **pillar of cloud and stood in the door of the tabernacle and called Aaron and Miriam to come forward.** (Numbers 12:4-5) God told them, He had always spoken to His prophets in visions and dreams or appeared as something other than

Himself. But, with His servant Moses, it was different! God spoke with Moses face to face! Then God told them not to speak against Moses.

The anger of the Lord was aroused against them and He departed. (Numbers 12:9)

He was so angry, He left them standing there! Speechless! When Aaron finally looked over at Miriam, she was a leper! She would be an outcast! She could not live among the people, she would be left behind! What would become of her?!

Moses interceded on her behalf and God lifted the leprosy from Miriam, but she was to be put out of the camp away from all the people for seven days.

We never again read anything about Miriam until her death about twenty years later. (Numbers 20:1) Did she learn her lesson? Did she continue to serve God, in a quiet, obedient way? We are not told.

If Miriam could send us a message, what would she say to us?

When you are given a work to do, do it and do not let jealousy and envy rule you. **Wrath is cruel and anger a torment, but who is able to stand before jealousy?** (Proverbs 27:4)

FOOD FOR THOUGHT

1. What is the description of a person who does not listen to and live by the words of Jesus Christ?
   1 Timothy 6:3-5

2. What does God think of envy?
   Romans 1:28-30

3. When we eliminate the sinful traits in our lives, with what should we then fill ourselves?
   Galatians 5:22-26

SONG   PURER IN HEART OF GOD

CHAPTER TEN

RAHAB

Joshua 2 & 6

The year is 1405 B.C. Moses had brought the Children of Israel to the border of Canaan and God appointed Joshua to take the children of Israel across the border and claim their promised land. Joshua sent two men to go into the city of Jericho, see what it looked like so Joshua could make a plan to take the city.

When the men got to Jericho, they found a place of lodging owned by a woman named Rahab. As it turned out, she was a harlot! Someone told the king of Jericho there were two strange men wandering around the city and they were lodging with Rahab.

The king told Rahab to turn the two men over to him, but instead she hid them. The kings men searched her house but did not find the two men. Why did she do that?

She along with all the people in the land had heard about the Israelites coming. She had heard about their God and the things He had done. He had dried up the Red Sea so His people could cross on dry land; and then He had drown all the Egyptians who had meant to harm them. Their God had fed them in the wilderness with manna from heaven and them water in the desert. She had heard about the Israelites defeating and destroying their enemies on the way to Jericho!

She was convinced **The Lord, your God, He is God in heaven above and on earth below** (Joshua 2:11) We know you are coming to take our land and destroy our people! We have been expecting you! The city has already been making preparation for war. Since I have protected you, will you protect me and my family when you come to destroy us?

An agreement was made. She will help them escape and then mark her house with a scarlet cord hanging from her window. Her house and all her family would be spared.

That red cord was a symbol of her hope! Hope of rescue! Hope of being saved! Hope for a future!

Her house was built on top of the city's wall. So, she let the men down the outer wall by that cord and they ran to the hills and hid until it was safe to go back to Joshua.

Rahab got all her family together, gathered provisions and prepared for the war to come. Her city was locked down! No one in! No one out! The enemy was coming

About a month later they came! But it sure wasn't what the people of Jericho thought it would be! Open your Bibles to Joshua chapter six. It was more, a war on nerves! For six days Rahab watched the armed Israelites march around her city. Nothing else! Just once a day, march around her city! On the seventh day, they came again, but this time they blew trumpets and shouted a loud war cry and the wall fell down flat! The whole wall all the way around her city!....except the section with her scarlet cord hanging from the window! The army went into the city and completely destroyed all that was in the city. Rahab and her family were brought out and they burned the city and everything in it, the only things they saved were items of silver, gold, bronze and iron.

Joshua spared Rahab the harlot, her father's household and all he had. So she dwells in Israel to this day, because she hid the messengers whom Joshua sent to spy out Jericho (Joshua 6:12-25)

Her hope was realized! Rescue!

We hear about Rahab several more times in Scripture:

Rahab is one of only four women named in the linage of Jesus the Christ. (Matthew 1:5)

Rahab's name comes up again, in the well known "Heroes of Faith" list. (Hebrews 11:31)

Another descendant of hers', James, the brother of Jesus, wrote: **Likewise was not Rahab the Harlot also justified by works, when she received the messengers and sent them another way?** (James 2:25)

But this is not the end of Rahab's story! Guess who her son was? We'll learn more about that in another lesson.

What is the message Rahab is sending us?

No matter what bad things come, (and they will!) Never give up hope! Prepare yourself for battle! Salvation is coming!

Looking for the blessed hope and glorious appearance of our God and Savior Jesus Christ (Titus 2:13)

FOOD FOR THOUGHT

1. Are you hanging on to your cord of hope? What are you hoping for? Can Jesus see you cord of hope? Can your friends see your cord of hope?

2. Where does hope come from?
   Romans 5:1-5   Romans 15:4

3. What does your hope look like?
   Galatians 5:22-26

4. Now that you have hope of deliverance, how can you, like Rahab, prepare yourself for when the hard times comes?
   Ephesians 6: 10-20

SONG   **MY HOPE IS BUILT ON NOTHING LESS**

CHAPTER ELEVEN

DEBORAH

Judges 4 & 5

Now Deborah, a prophetess, the wife of Lapidoth was judging Israel at the time. (Judges 4:4)

What was a prophetess or a prophet? A person, chosen by God to deliver his messages and instructions to the people.

What was a judge at that time? The office of judge was two fold. God appointed one judge to be the chief judicial officer he, or she, was to keep the peace among the Israelites, and be was the commander in chief of the Lord's army. He was to subdue the Canaanites and make the land of Canaan into the home of the Israelites. Now there were many tribes of people in Canaan but they were all Canaanites.

This was to fulfill the promise given to Abraham. God said I will give you this Land, and He did! Joshua won the battles and they subdued the land and the Canaanites feared the Israelites. The children of Israel were to be a people set apart for the Lord, and God had given them Canaan for their new home land.

But they never finished the job! There were always just enough of the Canaanites there to draw the people away from God. The twelve tribes of Israel could never quite be faithful to God! And when things would get so bad, the people would cry out for God to save them, and God would appoint a judge to bring peace to their land again. Then after twenty, thirty or forty years, the people would again begin running after other gods and things would go bad again!

Deborah was a prophetess, a judge and a warrior! She was the forth judge and at this time, Jabin was the king of the Canaanites and he had been oppressing the Israelites for twenty years when Deborah received instructions from the Lord to deploy troops at Mt. Tabor. Take ten thousand men **and against you I will deploy Sisera, the commander of Jabin's army, with his chariots and his multitude at the River Kishon; and I will deliver him to your hand.** (Judges 4:6-7)

So, she sent for her chief officer, Barak, and told him what God instructed. Barak said, I'll go if you do!

I will go with you, but if I do, the final victory will not belong to you, but to a woman. But..... she was not talking about herself! Deborah went with him and Barak took ten thousand men under his command and went to the top of Mount Tabor and from the top of the mountain, he looked down and saw Sisera was already there, ready for battle.

Deborah said **Up! For this is the day in which the Lord has given Sis'era into your hands.** (Joshua 4:14) and Barak went down from Mt. Tabor with his men and the Lord went before them and brought disorder to Sisera and all his army and they all fell before Barak. All except the coward, Sisera! He ran!

Sis'era came to a tent of a woman named Jael, who took him in and gave him milk to drink and a bed to rest.

And while he was sleeping, she drove a tent peg through his temple! He was defeated by a woman!

So on that day, God brought King Jabin of Canaan into submission in the presence of the children of Israel.

Under the leadership of Debra, the children of Israel grew **stronger and stronger until they destroyed Jabin king of Canaan.** (Joshua 4:21-24)

Then the celebration began! Deborah and Barak sang a song of victory, brought by the hand of the Lord! It began:

When leaders lead in Israel,
When the people willingly offer themselves,
Bless the Lord!

And it ended:

Thus let all your enemies perish,O Lord!
But let those who love Him be like the sun
When it comes out in full strength.

(Joshua 5:2-31)

So the land had rest for forty years.

What would be Deborah's message to us?

When you go willingly into battle, letting the Lord lead you and tell you what to do, you will win! Every time! And your life will be better for the battle! Then celebrate the Lord's victory!

Be faithful unto death and I will give you the crown of life (Revelation 2:10)

FOOD FOR THOUGHT

1. Deborah was willing to do battle for the Lord. Are our battles physical or spiritual today?
   Ephesians 3:14-21   Ephesians 6:10-12   Romans 8:37-39

2. Who will help us fight our battles?
   Isaiah 41:10-13   Philippians 4:13
   Colossians 1:11

3. Do friends, neighbors, co-workers, even family give you a hard time because you "go to church" instead of going with them? Do they make snide remarks or put down the church or Christ? Do if they accuse you of being a "goody-goody" person.
   1Peter 3:13-16   John 15:18   1John 3:13
   Philippians 1:27-29

4. Deborah prepared herself for battle. How can we prepare ourselves for the battles to come in our lives?
   Ephesians 6:13-17   James 1:12   Joshua 24:15
   1 Corinthians 16:13

SONG   **THE BATTLE BELONGS TO THE LORD**

CHAPTER TWELVE

RUTH AND NAOMI

Book of Ruth

Now it came to pass in the days when the judges ruled, that here was a famine in the land. And a certain man of Bethlehem, Judah, went to sojourn in the country of Moab, he and his wife and his two sons. (Ruth 1:1)

There is no way to tell the story of Ruth without telling the story of Naomi. We first start with Naomi's husband Elimelech.

When the famine came, Elimelech took his family from their homeland, where the people, at least in their village, still worshiped the One True God, and moved them to a place of false gods. A place where no altar had been built to honor or worship the Lord God. The people of Moab worshiped the Baal of Peor (Numbers 25:3-5) There were a lot of gods named Baal scattered throughout Canaan, they were named for their location; this one was at Mt. Peor.

How long they were in Moab before Elemeleck died, we don't know, but at some point, both boys married women of Moab and then, both boys died! This left three women with no man to provide for them.

Somehow, Naomi heard the Lord had provided for her people back in Bethlehem and she made arrangements to go home. She advised her daughters-in-law to return to their families and remarry. Opah sadly left Naomi and went back.

Ruth chose to go with Naomi. Had Ruth seen something different in Naomi? Something different from her people?

Open you Bible and read with me, Ruth 1:16-17. When we read these beautiful words, we see the love Ruth had for Naomi and the beginnings of faith in the God of Naomi. "Please don't ask me to go back. I want to go with you. I want to be part of your people and I want to worship your God." And so, Naomi and Ruth make the journey to Bethlehem.

Evidently, all those years away from home, at least ten years, Naomi did her best to remain faithful to the Lord God. But....when they reach Naomi's home, word got out she was back and all the city was excited to see Naomi home again! They called out to her, Naomi! Naomi! Is this Naomi back again?

In her native language, her name, Naomi translated Delight. Isn't that beautiful? A wonderful, joy filled name! But now she tells her friends, **Do not call me Naomi, call me Mara** (Bitter) **for the Almighty has dealt very bitterly with me. I went out full, and the Lord has brought me home again empty. Why do you call me Naomi since the Lord has testified against me and the Almighty has afflicted me?** (Ruth1:20-21) Naomi blamed God for all her troubles! Who made the decision to leave home where God was worshiped? Who made the decision to go to Moab, knowing it was a country where Baal was worshiped and God was not allowed? Other people, her friends and neighbors stayed home and depended on God to get them through the hard times. And He did! Why did her husband and sons die in that place? We are not told, chances are, because they refused to worship Baal, but would not go home. Was It was more important to live physically comfortable, than to live spiritually comfortable? We don't know. whatever happened, Naomi blamed God! And she continued to blame God!

It was the beginning of barley harvest, late April, when the two women reached Bethlehem and Ruth asked Naomi for permission to go into the fields and "glean" so the two of them would have food to eat.

Under Jewish law, the corners of the fields was not be harvested by the owners. And if their hired workers missed a patch of grain, they could not go back and harvest it. This was to be left standing in the fields for the poor to "glean". That was what Ruth wanted to do for herself and Naomi.

The owner of the field, a man by the name of Boaz, noticed Ruth and asked who she was. His servant explained she was the daughter-in-law of Naomi, the one who just came back home. Boaz knew Naomi; they were related by marriage, so he went to Ruth and advised her to stay in his fields next to the young women who worked for him. Then he told the men who worked for him, to leave Ruth alone. He provided noon meals for her just as he did for his workers and gave instructions to his workers to deliberately leave plenty of grain for her to find.

When the day was over, she took what she had gleaned plus part of her lunch, she had saved, back to Naomi. When Naomi asked, Ruth told her, she had been gleaning in the fields of a man name Boaz. And Ruth continued to glean in his fields through the barley season and on through the wheat season, until the end of August or September.

Just before harvest was over, Naomi explained to Ruth the meaning of "kinsmen redeemer" (Leviticus 25:23-55)

If a man died before he had a son, his inheritance returned back to his tribe. (the twelve tribes of Israel). Each tribe had its own land, it was divided up among the families of that tribe and could not be sold to anyone outside the tribe. The widowed wife was to marry the dead man's closest relative; a brother, cousin, uncle, and the new husband would be her kinsman redeemer. He would buy back the inheritance and give it to her, and when their first son was born, it would be for him and his descendants. Occasionally a man would refuse to be a kinsman redeemer and the duty would fall on the next closest male relative.

Naomi went on to explain the custom of how Ruth should let Boaz know she was ready to end her widowhood. It seems very unconventional to us, but Ruth was to go at the end of the last day of the wheat threshing when the season was over; the last meal eaten and the owner was asleep on the floor by his grain until he took it to storage the next day. After everyone else was gone, she was to go lay at his feet and when he woke, she would ask him to be her kinsman redeemer. So at midnight, she went quietly and laid at the feet of the sleeping Boaz. When he woke, she said **I am Ruth, your maidservant. Take your maidservant under your wing, for you are a near kinsman.** (Ruth 3:9) She was not offering to have sex with him, she was asking him to buy back her first husbands property for their first born son.

Boaz was more than willing to take on the responsibility, but....there was one problem. He was not the nearest relative. Boaz went the next morning and talked to the nearest kinsman, and explained who Ruth was what and what inheritance was to be bought. For whatever reason, this man did not want to redeem the inheritance of Chilion, the son of Naomi and husband of Ruth.

That left Boaz free to be her kinsman redeemer. The marriage took place and a son was born!

The neighbor women were so excited for Naomi! **the neighbor women gave him a name. And they called his name Obed** (Ruth 4:14-17)

We read no more about Ruth or Naomi, but this is not the end of Ruth's story. Her son, Obed gave her a great-grandson named David, who became King of Israel! Through whom came OUR REDEEMER, Jesus the Messiah!(Matthew 1:5:16 Luke 3:23,32)

As for Boaz, the great-grandfather of King David, He was the son of Rahab! (Matthew 1:5)

Looking for the blessed hope and glorious appearing of our great God and Savior Jesus Christ, who gave Himself for us, that He might redeem us from every lawless deed.

(Titus 2:14)

What is Ruth's message to us? It is very plain, loud and clear!

Have a heart that is willing to learn the truth, and love and obey God!**And you shall know the truth and the truth shall set you free!** John 8:32

1. Like Naomi, so you dwell on your problems rather than your blessings? Make a list of your blessings, big and small. Take your time, look for things you haven't recognized as blessings from God. James 1:17

2. Like Ruth, are you willing to walk away from things that stand between you and God? What did Ruth walk away from? Luke 18:28-30

3. Like Ruth, have you been Redeemed? Luke 1:68-69 Galatians 3:13 1Peter 1:18-19

SONG   **REDEEMED**

CHAPTER THIRTEEN

DELILAH

Judges 16:4-21

Y ou can not tell Delilah's story without telling the story of Samson, so let's back up a little. Read Judges 13:1-5. Before his birth, Samson was chosen by God to be a Judge of Israel.

What was a judge at that time? The office of judge was two fold. God appointed one judge at a time to be the chief judical officer (he was to keep peace among the Israelites) and he was the commander in chief of the Lords army. He was subdue the Canaanites and make the land of Canaan the home of the Israelites.

This was to fulfill the promise given to Abraham. God said I will give you this Land, and He did! They were there and the Canaanites feared the Israelites. They were a people set apart for the Lord. Their own home land.

The problem was, there have been six judges before Samson and each one of them failed to permanently subdue the ungodly people who lived there!

The Philistines were one of the tribes in Canaan and were a thorn in the flesh of the Israelites since the days of Abraham, because God's people would never fight hard enough, long enough to really destroy their enemy! And gradually, over time, God's people became more and more like their enemy; worshiping and serving false gods.

Now it's time for Samson, the last judge of Israel to stand up for God!

Before Delilah came into his life, Samson had already made two bad choices with women, both Philistines. His parents had warned him about choosing as woman, not of God's people, but he would not listen.

For twenty years he was carrying out God's instructions and he was, with God's help destroying the enemy! He had set fire to all their crops and vineyards and olive groves! He had killed a thousand Philistines at one time all by himself! He alone, pulled down the city gates, bar and all! and walked off with them! He had to be stopped!

The first woman betrayed him during their wedding feast! They were not married a week before Samson gave her to another man. (Judges 14:1-3)

The second woman was a harlot used as bate to trap Samson, and he walked right into it! But with God's help, he escaped! (Judges 16:1-3)

Both times the Philistines were trying to kill Samson because of his super human strength and all the destruction he had brought on them. But Samson was still walking around a free man!

Enter Delilah. (Judges 16:4-21) We know two things about her: Samson loved her and she was a Philistine.

We are never told they were married. We are told, she was waiting on Samson. Already had plans made to trap him. She had agreed to deliver him to the lords of the Philistines, and each one of them would pay her eleven hundred pieces of silver. We are told there were five lords of the Philistines (Judges 13:3) So that comes to about one hundred and ten thousand dollars in today's money.

Evidently she had a huge room in her house partitioned off into separate spaces (closets), for while she was entertaining Samson, men were hiding in another part of the room. All she had to do was entice him and find out the source of his strength.

And Delilah played her part! Can't you just see her? All made up and purring like a kitten? **Please tell me where your great strength lies, and with what you may be bound to afflict you.** (Judges 16:6)

Had Samson already learned his lesson? Did he get up right then and leave?

Sadly...no. He fabricated a story. Tie me up with seven fresh bowstrings, and I shall be as weak as any other man. He allowed her to tie him up! And the men were waiting for her signal! **The Philistines are upon you, Samson!** (Judges 16:9) And she ran out of the way to watch him be captured and collect her money!

But Samson easily broke loose.

Did she apologize for here betrayal? Beg his forgiveness? No! Delilah berated him for making fun of her! How dare you tell me lies! Please tell me the truth.

Why didn't Samson say "Goodby" and leave? But he didn't. Again, he concocted a story. This time it was new ropes. And again, Delilah tied him up and again gave the signal to the men waiting in the room. Again, he broke loose is if tied with thread!

A third time she berated him for lying to her and then begged him to tell her the truth. And again, another far-fetched story. He told her to weave his hair into the loom! And when he went to sleep, she did the deed. Again she called out the signal! But, he woke up and pulled loose.

How can you say "I love you" when your heart is not with me? You have mocked me these three times and have not told me where your great strength lies. (Joshua 16:15)

Verse sixteen tells us she pestered him daily, until she worried him to death! Why didn't he just leave? She was after him continually for days until he finally told her the truth! His strength was in his hair that had never been cut. Why?!? Why did he tell her?

We are told, this time she knew he told her her truth. So Delilah called the Philistines one more time and told them to be sure to bring her money!

Evidently Delilah drugged him and "lulled" him to sleep, cut off his hair and then she tormented him. How? Did she whisper in his ear? Now I've got you, Samson. I will have my money and be rid of you. You will pay for trying to destroy my people.

Again, she gave the signal and Samson woke up and thought I will be just fine, just like all the other other times, but then he realized; **the Lord had departed from him. Then the Philistines took him, put out his eyes and took him down to Gaza** (Judges16: 20-21) They used him as an ox to turn the grinding wheel in the prison mill.

Time passed and Samson's hair was growing out, but his strength did not come back, for the Lord was not with him.

The day came for all the Philistines to go to their temple and make a sacrifice to their god, Dagon. His image was a torso of a man with the head of a fish. A hideous thing to behold! It was a day of feasting and drinking. **So it happened when their hearts were merry, that they said. Call for Samson, that he may perform for us.**(Judges16:25) They wanted to torment this man, who was once a strong warrior, and now he was a blind man living and working like an animal.

The temple was full of men and women and there were three thousand more up on the roof! Picture an open second story overlooking the large courtyard below. Historians estimate there were a total of eight to ten thousand people there! Was Delilah there?

Samson was led by a young boy, into the courtyard of the temple of Dagon and it was there Samson finally called on his God. He turned back to God! He asked God for help! He was depending on God again! **O Lord God, remember me, I pray, just this once O God that I may with one blow take vengeance on the Philistines for my two eyes!** (Judges 16:30) Did Delilah hear him calling on the One True God of Israel?

Samson told the boy to place him between the two middle supporting pillars of the temple. One more call on his Lord and then with all the strength the Lord could supply, Sampson pushed on the pillars with all his might and the temple fell on the Philistine lords and all the people! The last words of Samson were **Let me die with the Philistines!** (Judges 16:30) More enemies of God were destroying at one time than in all the battles Samson had fought put together!

What happened to Delilah? Was she there? What were her last thoughts? Confusion? Regrets? Fear? Calling on Dagon?

Did she finally acknowledge the power of Samson's God?

What would be her message to us?

No god can stand before the Lord God! Money will not protect you! Nor will money buy safety or happiness! You do not want to know the extent of the wrath of God!

For the wrath of God is revealed from heaven against all ungodliness and unrighteousness of men, who suppress the truth in unrighteousness. (Romans 1:18)

FOOD FOR THOUGHT

1. If we, like Samson choose to associate with ungodly people, what will be the result?

    Proverbs 12:26   Proverbs 17:15   1Timothy 5:22
                      2 Corinthians 6:14-18

2. Do you know someone, who, like Delilah would be willing to do something wrong if rewarded with a lot of money?

    1 Timothy 6:10

3. Delilah had the wrong priorities. Samson seemed to have forgotten his priorities. What are your priorities?
    Wealth? Romance? To be boss? Popularity?
    What about God? His Son, Jesus? Is He number one? Absolutely? No exceptions?

    Exodus 20:25   Matthew 6:33   John14:6   Colossians 2:6-9

SONG **I'D RATHER HAVE JESUS**

CHAPTER FOURTEEN

HANNAH

1 Samuel 1 & 2

The year was around B.C.1105. For the most part the Israelites were an unruly, sinful people. They were constantly trying to combine worship to God (when they were in desperate need) with worship to false gods. When the last judge, Samson, died, the Lord was still using prophets to try to guide His people. But we read several times toward the end of the book of Judges "In those days there was no kng in Israel". The twelve tribes of Israel just could not get along! Finally, they turned on each other and went their separate ways. **In those days there was no king in Israel; everyone did what was right in his own eyes.** (Judges 21:25) They refused to listen and follow the judges and accept God as their authority and their King.

There were still a few good people trying to serve and obey the One True God. One such man was named Elkana. **This man went up from his city yearly to worship and sacrifice to the Lord of hosts in Shiloh.** (1Samuel 1:3) This was before the first temple was built and the faithful still went to the tabernacle (tent) that Moses instituted when God gave him the Law.

This was a special, one time a year holiday. A grand feast! (Think Christmas or Thanksgiving for us.) All those special food prepared once a year! When Elkana made preparations for his sacrifice and feast, he had portions prepared for each member of his family. But, there was a problem....

Elkana had two wives. It was never God's intent for a man to have two wives. He cannot be faithful to two women. Both cannot be equal in his affections. It is not possible. But, like most of his socitey, Elkana had two wives. Peninnah, who gave him children and Hannah was barren. But, Elkana made no secret of the fact that Hannah was the one he loved and treated special. Even on this special, once a year holiday, he showed his preference. He always had a double portion of the feast prepared for her. And that was the problem. Out of jealousy, Peninnah went out of her way to give Hannah a hard time, especially on these holidays! After all, she had given Elkana children, and she deserved first place! (sound familiar?)

Every year, when they went to the house of the Lord, she deliberately made Hannah's day horrible! Hannah would be so upset, she could not eat anything, much less enjoy the day. This year, it was so bad, Hannah got up, went to the doorstep of the deserted tabernacle and cried her heart out! **Oh Lord of Hosts, if you will have compassion on me and give me a male child, then I will give him to the Lord all the days of his life.** (1Samuel1:11) She also promised her son would keep the Nazarite vow all the days of his life. This child would be dedicated to serve the purposes of God. His hair would never be cut and he would never eat grapes, or anything made from grapes. (Numbers 6:1-6) Usually, men took this vow for a specific number of days or months, or until a deed or work was accomplished. For Hannah's son, it would be for a lifetime. Sampson (Judges 13:1-5) and John the baptizer (Luke 1:13-15) were both under the Nazarite vow for a life time.

While Hannah was praying, the priest, Eli came to her and assured her, God heard her prayer. She had finally emptied her soul to God and He gave her peace! She left the tabernacle a different person!

Then we read, **Hannah conceived and bore a son and named him Samuel. Because I have asked for him from the Lord.** (1Samuel

1:20) Could it be because she did finally turn to God for help? Maybe she should have gone to God for help earlier. Hannah finally had her son! She told her husband she would not be going back for the yearly feast and sacrifice until Samuel was weaned, sometime between three and five years old. Babies were nursed much longer, even up into the nineteen hundreds, when baby formula and foods were made available.

When the time came, Hannah went with her family back to the tabernacle for the feast and sacrifice. And she gave her son into the care of Eli, the priest. She never brought her son home again!

Every year Hannah went back for the feast and time of worship, and every year she brought a new robe for her son. Don't you know that was a grand, special robe? Do you think Samuel joined his family at these times? A happy family reunion every year!

We read the Lord blessed her with three more sons and two daughters, Her life of virtue and service reminds us of the woman of Proverbs 31:10-31

That is the last time we hear of Hannah, but what do you think was in her heart when she went to see her son and he told her, he and God had spoken to one another?!?

Years later, what did she think when Samuel told her the **Lord was with him and revealed Himself to Samuel in Shiloh by the word of the Lord.** (1Samuel 3:19-21) Samuel was now a prophet of the Lord.

Was Hannah still living when her son anointed the first king of Israel? (1Samuel 10:20-24) And years later, when he anointed the young man, David a king of Israel? (1Samuel 16:7-13) What a man of God her son grew to be!

What would Hannah's message be, to us, today?

Have enough faith to take your troubles to God! Do not try to fix your problems by yourself. Make God your first resort not your last!

Be anxious for nothing, but in everything by prayer and supplication, with thanksgiving, let your requests be made known to God. (Philippians 4:6)

FOOD FOR THOUGHT

1. Are you like Hannah, do you worry about things you have no control over?

    Psalm 29:11   1Peter 5:7   2Cortinthians 4:8-9

    Romans 15:13   Philippians 4:19

2. What did Hanna finally do?   1 Samuel 1:10

3. Do you spend time in prayer? Other than meal time, just you and God? Or are you too busy?

    Isaiah65:24   Philippians4:6   1Thessalonians 5:17-18

    Hebrews 4:16   Psalm 91:15   Matthew 6:6

    Matthew 7:7-11

Make a study for yourself. (this could be my next book) Go through Paul's writings and read his prayers. Then study the prayers of David in Psalms

SONG   **SWEET HOUR OF PRAYER**

CHAPTER FIFTEEN

MICHAL

1 Samuel 18:20 through 25:44
2 Samuel chapter1 through 6

Michael was a princess, the younger daughter of Saul, the first king of Israel. She had three brothers and one sister. And she loved the heart-throb of Israel! The young David! Good looking! A musician! A strong athlete! A fearless warrior! And he was a faithful worshiper of God! The people of Israel were even singing a folk song about him!

Over time, Michal's father had shown himself to be selfish, disobedient toward God, a deceiver, and now he was jealous of young David. As time went by, Saul's jealousy grew. How to discredit this kid or get rid of him?

Saul had a foolproof plan.

I will give her (Michal) **to him, that she may be a snare to him and the hand of the Philistines may be against him.** (1Samuel 18:21) Israel's enemy, the Philistines, knew who David was; he had killed their national hero, Goliath. They would be glad to kill David. And to make sure his plan worked, King Saul would ask for a very unusual dowry for his daughter!Not the ordinary livestock or possessions....just one hundred dead Philistines! David would die in the attempt!

So David agreed and went to war to win his bride. He came home with proof of not one hundred dead Philistines, but two hundred! Saul's plan didn't work, but Michal got her wish!

But things went down hill from there. Saul had to get rid of Michal's new husband! It became an obsession. But the people could not know. If the people knew Saul would be responsible for David's death, there would be an insurrection! So he very quietly ordered his servants to kill David when he came to the palace. Michal found out and David didn't go!

Saul arranged for assassins to go to Michal and David's house and kill him in his sleep. Michal found out and helped David escape.

Now Saul was really mad! From that time on, he never ceased trying to kill his son-in-law. And he didn't care who knew it!

Michal's husband was running for his life. He was declared an outlaw and the army of Israel, under the command of Abner, was sent after him. David was soon seen as the champion of the down trodden, think Robin Hood. All the people who the king disliked, for whatever reason, packed up their families and went to join David. His own father and all his family came to him.

Soon David had an army and was fighting the enemies of Israel! He was in truth, helping Saul and David never raised a hand against his father-in-law, the Lord's anointed king.(1Samuel 24:2-10, 36:2-11) He was even protecting Saul! It would be several years before Michal saw her husband again. Others went to join him, why didn't she? Did Michal miss David? Still love him?

The next time we hear of Michal, her father gave her to another man! Did she get tired of waiting for David, or was this just another of her father's schemes?(1 Samuel 25:44)

David's popularity kept growing and Saul's could not win against the Philistines. Battle after battle, until finally, they killed King Saul and his sons. With Saul dead, the Lord told David to go Judah, the tribes of Israel who refused to be ruled by Saul. The leadership of

Judah, "the House of Judah" anointed David king and Judah became the "House of David".

Abner, the commander of Saul's army anointed Saul's last son as king of Israel. Still the "House of Saul". After years of war between the two, and Judah growing stronger and Israel growing weaker, finally, Abner was through. He could not win with God always on David's side. So he went to David with a proposition. Make a treaty with me and I will help you take the land of Israel. David's answer? On one condition......Get my wife back for me.(2Samuel 3:13)

Michal was sent for and Abner sent word to the leaders or Israel. For a long time you have wanted David to be your king. Now is the time. **Now then, do it! For the Lord has spoken of David saying, by the hand of My servant David, I will save My people, Israel from the hand of the Philistines and the hand of all their enemies.** (2 Samuel 3:18)

About this time, Ishbosheth, the last son of Saul was murdered.

The leaders of Israel and Judah joined as one nation and made David king! A United Israel, for the first time! And Jerusalem is now the City of David and Michal is the queen of all Israel! The Lord God was with David and he became great. (2Samuel 5:6-10)

The next time we see Michal, she is standing at her window, looking out at the street below. There is a nation wide celebration that day. All of Israel is celebrating the return of the long lost Ark of the Covenant! It was recovered from their enemies and home in Israel again. Time to celebrate! David was out with his people, celebrating and the first thing he did was offer a sacrifice to God. Then singing and dancing to the Lord as the Ark is paraded through the streets on the way to the tabernacle of the Lord. David offered another sacrifice to the Lord and a peace offering and he blessed the people in the name of the Lord, and provided a feast for every one!

Michal, Saul's daughter looked through a window and saw King David leaping and whirling before the Lord and she despised him in her heart. (2Samuel 6:16)

David returned to his house and he was still in the attitude of worship and thanksgiving. As he entered the door, Michal came to him and falsely accused him of shaming the house of Saul! Did she forget? There is no house of Saul! God ended it because of Saul's disobedience!

And what did David do to bring shame? He took off his royal robes and put on an ephod! Was she accusing David of being nude? Would David have appeared nude to publicly worship his God? No. She was just accusing him of trying to attract the attention of the maids of his servants; the lowest social position there was, servants of servants by dressing like a commoner. Reducing himself! Forgetting his position, He was King!

David was a priest of the Lord God (1Samuel 30:7-8) and priests were not royalty, they were commoners.

SIDE NOTE When the priests worn an ephod, God commanded them to wear clothing under it, but it was said "they wore an ephod". You can read the full description of all the clothing a priest was to wear. (Exodus 28)

So, David took off the signs of royalty, dressed like a commoner and worshiped his God. How dare he?

It sounds like David was out of patience with her. Remember, David was a commoner! He was not born into a royal family. He was anointed king, and he was a priest and before that he was a warrior and before that he was a shepherd! He said to her: The Lord chose me instead of your father and He appointed me ruler over Israel. **Therefore I will play music before the Lord. And I will be even more undignified than this, and I will be humble in my own sight.** And the common people, including the servant's maids, will respect me. (2Samuel 6:21-22). David was not puffed up with his own importance, like Michal.

David was a follower of God first and king second.

The last time we hear of her, we are told a very sad fact. **Therefore Michal the daughter of Saul had no children to the day of her death,** (2Samuel 6:23) To an Israelite woman, this was a spiritual sign. Any time some one was sick, or defective in any way, it was believed it was because of sin in the life of the affected, so if a woman was unable to have children it was a sign of shame. Even if the accusation was untrue. In this case, God wanted the family line to end, so it was a true saying.

Michal's story raises a lot of questions.

Why was she so full of bitterness and hate? Did either of her husbands ever love her? Did her father ever love her?

When did the love she had for David turn to hate?

Did she allow her disappointment and hurt to turn her away from God, or did she ever have God in her life?

She could not accept the fact, the house of Saul had ended. She was the last of his children and she had no children. Did she blame God rather than her father who had tuned from God? Or did she blame David? Who never raised a hand against Saul?

If she could send us a message, what would it be?

Do not waste your life in bitterness and hate. Do not put your trust in your position or things of this world.

Command those who are rich in this present age not to be haughty, nor to trust in uncertain riches, but in the living God, who gives us richly all things to enjoy. (1Timothy 6:17)

FOOD FOR THOUGHT

1. Which is more important in your life? Things you own? Your place in society? Your relationship with God?

2. When things go wrong in our lives, is it ever our fault?
   1 Corinthians 13:5

3. If you find yourself blaming God, or blaming others, what should you do?

   Proverbs 3:5-6   Proverbs 12:15   Matthew 7:3-5
                        Romans 2:1

4. If the "glow" is gone out of a relationship you have with your husband, your sister, your mother, your best friend; what should you do?

   Ephesians 4:31,32   Matthew 7:12   Romans 14:10-13
            Philippians 4:7   Proverbs 10:12

SONG   IS THY HEART RIGHT WITH GOD

CHAPTER SIXTEEN

ABIGAIL

1Samuel 25:2-42

Abigail is described as **a woman of good understanding and beautiful apperance; but the man** (her husband) **was harsh and evil in his doings** (1 Samuel 25:3)

Good judgment, smart, wise and she was beautiful. She was also married to a very rich, but harsh, mean, dishonest man.

This was during the time David was on the run from Saul. He had six hundred warriors and their families and many other people who had fled from King Saul. They all depended on David for their livelihood. David knew a rancher not far away who was sheering his sheep and butchering the meat so he sent one of his men with a request: "The whole time your shepherds were up in the hills with your sheep, we protected them from the Philistines. You didn't loose one animal. Now could you please give us few of your sheep to feed our families?"

The man who owned the sheep was Nabal, Abigail's husband. He had three thousand sheep and a thousand goats. And his answer was.... "No! David is an outcast! A runaway servant of the king!. And I don't know who you are. My sheep are for my servants."

When they went back and told David, he told four hundred men to arm themselves and get ready to go get the meat.

One of Nabal's men overheard the conversation and went to Abigail. He told her how David's men had protected them and their flocks up in the hills, day and might, the whole time they had the sheep in high pastures. And now, David has asked for some meat for his people and your husband refused! David and some of his men are coming and there is going to be trouble! **He** (Nabal) **is such a scoundrel that one cannot speak to him**. (1 Samuel 25:16-17)

Abigail, trying to protect her husband, took matters into her own hands. She took supplies to feed David and all his people and begged him to reconsider. The Lord will make you a long lasting dynasty because you fight for Him and you are a good man. Please forgive me for interfering, but our workers are willing to help you and you do not want to shed innocent blood over this thing, it will bring you grief.

David listened to Abigail and said it was a blessed day because she came to him. David then thanked her for her advice, and for keeping him **from avenging myself with my own hand**. (1Samuel 25:33-34) because by morning, no man would have been left alive!

He sent Abilgail home with the promise that no harm would come to her, her husband or her people.

She had stopped a catastrophe! Her husband and all their workers and flocks could have been destroyed! When she got home, Abigail found her husband throwing a big party, worthy of a king! And he was so drunk, she couldn't talk to him and tell him what happened!

When Nabal sobered up enough the next morning to listen to her, she told him of his near escape and the man went into shock! A stroke that left him paralyzed! Ten days later the Lord struck Nabal, and he died.

When David heard of Nabal's death, he sent word of marriage proposal to Abigail. She said she was willing to go to him as a servant. The lowest position in the household! The servant who washed the feet of the other servants! Before you judge David to harshly, remember, his former father-in-law gave his wife to another man.

Then we are told she was married to David. (1Samuel 25:42)

We read her name one more time, in the genealogy of David. She is listed as the mother of his son, Daniel. (1 Chronicles 3:1)

What would be Abigail's message to us?

Instead of adding wood to the fire, put the fire out! Be a peacemaker instead of a trouble maker!

Blessed are the peace makers, for they shall be called sons (children) **of God** (Matthew 5:9)

FOOD FOR THOUGHT

1. David admitted to Abigail, he was wrong to think about taking vengeance. Are you ever tempted to "get even"?
   Hebrews 10:30   Deuteronomy 32:35
   Matthew 5:22-26

2. If you did "get even", would you be willing to try to restore the relationship with the one you offended and your relationship with God?
   James 5:16   1John1:9

3. Would you be willing, like Abigail, to be used by God, to step up and try to help solve a problem and bring peace between two people, even if the one in the wrong is a friend or family member?
   Matthew 5:9   Galatians 6:1-2

SONG   HE WHISPERS SWEET PEACE TO ME

CHAPTER SEVENTEEN

JEZEBEL

1Kings 16:30 – 22:1-53   2Kings chapters 1 & 9
2 Chronicles 21:18-20, 22:1-12

NOTE: Research and tradition tells us, the prophet Jeremiah wrote the books of Kings and the prophet Ezra wrote the books of Chronicles. Each man was inspired of God, but they give us different details of the same events, and they sometimes spell names differently.

Before we tell her story, we need a bit of history first. God had set up the Kingdom of Israel, one kingdom. After the days of Abigail, our last story, a lot has happened. Abigail's husband, King David was a man after God's own heart, as was his son, Solomon **until his wives turned his heart after other gods; and his heart was not loyal to the Lord his God.** (1Kings11:4) Because of this, God told Solomon, his kingdom would would be divided but one tribe would be preserved **for the sake of my servant David, and for the sake of Jerusalem, which I have chosen.** (1 Kings11:13)

Remember the blessing Isaac gave his son Esau? His descendants, the Edomites would rebell against the descendents of his brother, Jacob and his son Judah? Read verse fourteen. Now the Lord raised up an adversary against Soloman: Hadad the Edomite and wars between Israel and Judah began. As evil as the kingdom of Israel became, so eventually did the kingdom of Judah!

Our story of Jezebel begins about about two hundred years after Soloman. And each king of Israel has been worse than the last, some ruled only a few months or only a few years and they were killed or died because of their wickedness. Then along comes Ahab, king of Israel and he **did evil in the sight of the Lord, more than all who were before him** Then we are told, he did the worst thing he ever did....**he took as wife Jezebel**! Then he went out and served Baal and worshiped him. (1Kings 16:30-31)

So, who was Jezebel? She was a princess; the daughter of Ethbaal, king of the Sidonians. To please her, Ahab built a temple and an altar to Baal. And he built Jezebel a palace of ivory! (1Kings 22:39)

Because of the wickedness of those two, God sent His prophet, Elijah, to the king with a message: There will be no rain, not even dew on your land for three years. Then God told Elijah to go hide!

Jezebel was so angry, she massacred all of prophets of God she could find! And she and Ahab sent men all over the country, looking for Elijah. A man named Obadiah hid one hundred of them in a cave. Meanwhile, Jezebel was entertaining, at her table, four hundred and fifty prophets of Baal and four hundred prophets of Asherah, the female Baal.

Then God told Elijah to go back to the king and have a contest between Baal and God, Himself. All the children of Israel, and all of Jezebel's prophets were to come to Mount Carmel. The prophets were to build an altar, prepare a sacrifice and petition Baal to send down fire to burn the sacrifice. From morning to evening, they did everything they could to get Baal to show himself. They leaped and danced around the altar. They cried aloud and cut themselves until their blood gushed out. They they prophesied until evening but Baal never came. (1 Kings 18:25-29)

Then Elijah built an altar, prepared a sacrifice and had water poured all over it, not once, but three times, so that even the trench around the altar was full of water. And then Elijah prayed. **Hear me, O Lord, hear me, that this people may know that You are the Lord God, and that You have turned their hearts back to You again.**(1Kings 18:37)

And God sent down fire and consumed the sacrifice, the water and the stones which were used to build the altar, even the dust that was left! And the people killed all of Jezebel's prophets!

And again, Jezebel was so angry, she sent men to find Elijah and kill him! Time passes and then King Ahab decided he wanted a vineyard that belonged to another man. He had no right to it. He just wanted it.

It belonged to man named Naboth whose land was bordered by the wall of Jazreel in Sameria. and he did not want to sell it because it was his inheritance and would one day belong to his children.

This man, this king of Israel, was nothing more than a spoiled infant. **He lay down on his bed, and turned away his face and would eat no food** (1 Kings 21:4) Jezebel told him to get up, act like a king and be happy. I will get the vineyard for you. And she did. She had Naboth falsely accused of blaspheming God and the king, and then had him executed! Then she had the property taken from the family of Naboth and gave it to the king!

She used God, the Lord God of Israel as an excuse to murder a man and rob his family! (1Kings 21:9-13)

Finally God was out of patience with these two. Scripture says **He was provoked to anger.**(1Kings 21:22) He sent Elijah back to the king with an ominous message: Ahab and all his family, including Jezebel, will end! They will all die! Each member of the family would either be eaten by dogs or their blood would be licked up by dogs. To the children of Israel, nothing was lower than a dog. This would be the worst possible death for any person, but the royal family?!? The Jews always referred to their enemies as dogs.

There was no one like Ahab who sold himself to do wickedness in the sight of the Lord, because Jezebel his wife stirred him up. (1Kings 21:25) When Ahab heard this, he went into mourning, sackcloth and ashes. Evidently true repentance, for God showed him mercy. These things would not come to pass until after Ahab died.

And so it happened:

Ahab was killed in battle and dogs licked his blood from his chariot. (1Kings 22:34-38)

His son, Ahaziah. inherited the throne and then had an accident and never recovered from his injures. Instead of turning the Lord for help, he turned to Baal-Zebub! And God said Ahaziah would never get out of his bed again. (2Kings 1:2-4,17)

Ahab's next son, Jehoram (Joram), came to the throne. This was his last son by his wife, Jezebel. At this time, there were two kings with the same name. Ahab's son, the king of Israel and the king of Judah.

At this same time, the Lord God, had His prophet Elisha, appoint Jehu as the new king over Israel. One not of Ahab's family, because, by the hand of Jehu would come the end of Ahab's family.

Jehu sent for Joram for a meeting and Joram asked Jehu if there was a way they could make peace. The answer was: **What peace, as long as the harlotries of your mother Jezebel and her witchcraft are so many?** (2Kings 9:22) Joram could not defend his mother, so he proved himself a coward and turned and ran! But Jehu's arrow killed him. And his body was thrown into Naboth's field

When Jezebel was told of her last son's death, she did not dress in traditional mourning attire. Instead she painted her face, put on her crown and appeared at the window of her ivory palace as if to say, now I am the only ruler, the queen of Israel!

At that moment, two men pushed her out of her window and then calmly went to eat with the new king of Israel. When they went back to get her off the street and bury her, **they found no more of her than the skull and the feet and the palms of her hands.**(2 Kings 9:35) The dogs had eaten her! The pieces were gathered up and scattered over the field of Naboth by the wall of Jezreel, so there would be no place to find her grave.

Not long after her death, the last of Ahab's family were executed. (2Kings10:1-14) There were no more males in the family of Ahab to rule Israel.

So, Elijah's prophecies all came true. Why did God destroy this family?

But there was no one like Ahab who sold himself to do wickedness in the sight of the Lord because Jezebel his wife stirred him up. (1Kings 21:25) And because of them, their whole family was wicked. Those two caused the whole nation of Israel to sin in the Lord's sight!

This is the last we here of Jezebel, but......she had a daughter! Can you image a daughter raised by Ahab and Jezebel? Look how their son Ahaziah turned out.

Jezebel's daughter was named **Athaliah.** She was married to the King of Judah. Her husband was Jehoram and he was a wicked as the kings of Israel, just like his father-in-law, **for the daughter of Ahab was his wife.** (2 Kings 8:17-18) What does that tell you?

The Philistines and Arabians invaded Judah and the Kings house. They carried off all the kings possessions and all of his sons except his youngest one. Then the Lord struck Jehoram with an incurable disease **and to no one's sorrow, he died!** (2 Chronicles 21:18-20)

Athaliah had named her youngest son after her brother, Ahaziah. He reigned one year as king and he was killed because he chose to be as wicked as his mother's family! He was as wicked as all the rest of his family because his mother was his counselor!

When Athaliah received news that her last son was killed she destroyed all the royal heirs of the house of Judah. All of her son's nephews, cousins, any male however distantly related to any of her son, she had killed.

All but one. One of Athaliah's granddaughters took her baby brother and hid him in the Temple in Jerusalem and kept him hidden for six years and for six years Athaliah ruled as the only queen of Israel. (2 Chronicles 22:2-11)

When the little boy, Joash, was seven years old, the priests and the people made him king of Judah and they took Athaliah out and killed her! (2 Chronicles 23:5)

We hear no more of Athalia and the last we hear of Jezebel is found in the book of Revelation. Jesus was speaking to John the apostle and dictated a letter from Himself to the church in Ephesus. Part of that letter accused the church there of following the example of Jezebel and falsely teaching His **servants to commit sexual immorality and to eat things sacrificed to idols.** (Revelation 2:20)

I don't think we want to hear a message from Jezebel or her daughter! So, I will give you one.

Open you Bible with me and read, Joshua 24:1-16. Joshua told the people he had done all he could do to lead the Lord's people. God had fought and won battles for them and given them their new home with cities, vineyards and olive groves all ready in place. And still the people had trouble trusting, believing and staying faithful to God. They still turned to other gods. He, Joshua, had stayed faithful to God, when all the others had turned their backs on Him.

And then he said, **choose for yourselves this day, whom you shall serve, whether the gods which your fathers served. But as for me and my house, we will serve the Lord.** (Joshua 24:15)

FOOD FOR THOUGHT

1. How did Jezebel and her daughter stir up their families?

2. Jezebel and her daughter were manipulators, murderers and they hated God! They were the example of everything not to be! What example are we? What are people seeing, when they look at us?

   Galatians 5:19:26   Proverbs 31:10-3

3. What do you stir people up to do? You have influence on your husband, your children your grandchildren. How are you leading? What are you teaching? Did you ever stop to think, God gave these people into your care? You have a responsibility to them. One day, when they stand before God, what will they witness about you?

   Hebrews 10:24

SONG   A CHARGE TO KEEP I HAVE

CHAPTER EIGHTEEN

HULDA

2Kings 22:14-20   2Chronicles 34:22-25

I n the lesson we had on Deborah, we learned what a prophet was. One who received messages from God and delivered them to His people, because the people did not have copies of His law to live by.

Hulda was a prophet of the Lord during the time when Kings ruled in Judah. (She was also the namesake of my father's grandmother.) And ever since the time of Soloman's rule, each king did evil in the sight of the Lord, each one worse than the last.

Read 2 Kings 21:1-6 Manasseh was king of Israel and God's children were practicing witchcraft, using spiritists and mediums! His children were even sacrificing their children!. The king sacrificed his son to the false god, Molech! And he put images of false gods in the Lord's temple!

When he died, his son, Amon became king. Finally, King Amon was so wicked, his own servants in his own house killed him! His little son, Josiah, was only eight years old when he was made king.

He was the grandson of Athaliah, the baby who was hidden for seven years. This child knew about the Lord God of Israel through his grandfather, Adaiah, his mother's father who was a priest of God. **Josiah did what was right in the eyes of the Lord.**(2Kings 22:2)

When Josiah was twenty six years old, he ordered the temple of the Lord, Soloman's temple, to be repaired and in the process the long lost Book of Law was found! It was read to the king and when Josiah heard the words of Law, he went into mourning for his nation. Our fathers have not obeyed the words of the book and the wrath of the Lord is aroused against us. What do we need to do? He sent a servant to find a prophet of God. Go ask this prophet to **inquire of the Lord for me, for the people and for all of Judah, concerning the words of this book that has been found.** (2Kings 22:13)

The servant of the king went to Hulda, the prophetess who lived in Jerusalem.

The message she received from the Lord to be delivered to the king was two fold.

Because the people of Judah had become so wicked and were worshiping other gods, the Lord's wrath was going to come on them. Tell the man who sent you to me The Lord says He will bring calamity on this place and all the people.

The second part of the message was for Josiah, himself. **Thus says the Lord God of Israel: concerning the words which you have heard---Because your heart was tender and you humbled yourself before the Lord... and you tore your clothes and wept before Me, I also have heard you." says the Lord.** (2Kings 22:18-19) And the Lord had mercy on Josiah. Before the calamity was to come, Josiah would receive peace in death.

Josiah ruled five more years and the first thing he did was to bring all the rulers from all the parts of Judah to Jerusalem. Then he spoke to all the rulers and all the people of Jerusalem **All the people both small and great; and he read, in their hearing all the words of the Book of the Covenant.** (2Kings 23:1-2)

Then Josiah cleaned out all the idols that had been brought into the Lord's temple and removed all the evil priests. Then he went through all Judea and torn down all the evil places of worship. Read this chapter and see all the wickedness the kings before had instituted, encouraged and participated in! No wonder God was going to send His wrath!

Then Josiah restored the Passover for the first time since there were kings in Judah! Passover had not been kept since the time of Judges! Four hundred and ten years before!

There was no king like him, who turned to the Lord with all his heart, with all his soul, and with all his might according to all the Law of Moses, nor after him did any rise like him! (2 Kings 23:21-25)

And God kept his word delivered by Hulda.

God showed mercy for Josiah and he died before he saw his sons Jehoahaz and Eliakim (Jehoiakim) made kings of Judah one after the other, and who were wicked and did evil in the sight of the Lord as the kings who came before their father did. And they gave themselves to do the bidding of the Egyptian Pharaoh, Necho! God's mercy allowed Josiah to rest in peace before Nebuchadnezzar of Babylon conquered Judah and took the people of Judah away into captivity just twelve years after his death!

Some of your Bibles have maps in the back and some of them show the city of Jerusalem and the temple grounds. Inside the outer wall was a porch surrounding the temple, the Royal Porch. There were two gates on the south side called Hulda Gates. What a memorial to her!!!

Most of this story was not about Hulda, but the part she played, was very important! There had been before her and there would be after her, false prophets, who lie to the people, give them wrong information or not quite all the truth. She told the truth. The true message from the Lord. The good things to come and the bad things to come. The WHOLE truth!

What would be her message to us today? Be like Josiah! Read and know what the "word of the Lord" says. Then do it!

And be like Hannah! When you give someone information about the Bible, be sure it is the truth and the whole truth!

Beware of false prophets, who come to you in sheep's clothing, but inwardly they are ravenous wolves. (Matt7:15)

FOOD FOR THOUGHT

1. Are there prophets today? Paul tells us the gift of prophecy (receiving and delivering new words, new messages and new instructions from God) ended in the first century. God had inspired men to write the books and letters (the New Testament), and these writings were copied and it wasn't long before every congregation of the church in all the known world, had copies to read and study. There had been copies of the old writings (the Old Testament) for hundreds of years. By the end of the first century even some private individuals had copies. "That which was perfect had come": The Church Christ built and the written teachings of God and His Son were readily available to all people. (1Corinthians13:8) The book of Revelation was the last prophecy delivered to a man.

2. Today, we have teachers, who teach us what the Bible tells us. Are some of these people false teachers? What does a false teacher look like?

    1 Timothy 1:5-7   1 Timothy 4:1-5 2   Timothy 4:3-5
            2 Peter chapter 2   Matthew 15:8-9

3. What does the Bible say about witchcraft, spiritists and mediums?

    Deuteronomy 18:10-14   2 Kings 21:6   Micah 5:12
            Galatians 5:20

4. What does the Bible say about human sacrifice?

    Leviticus 18:21   2 Kings 17:17-18   Ezra 20:31
            Psalm 106:37-42

5. How can we know if a teacher is true or false? Does He teach the whole truth? Or leave somethings unsaid?

     Acts17:11 2   Timothy 2:15-19

6. Are you to tell someone else the story of Jesus and His salvation? Are you to teach others? When you do, do you, like Hannah, tell the whole truth, and not just what others want to hear?

     Matthew 15:7-9   2 Peter 2

SONG TRUE- HEARTED, WHOLE-HEARTED

CHAPTER NINETEEN

ESTHER

(Hadassah)
The Book of Esther

About a hundred and thirty years before our story begins, the Israelites had been captured and taken from their homeland and scattered to distant lands. Some had been taken to Persia. By the time of our story in 483 B.C., they had been in Persia about four generations. Now they were known as Jews and the Persians hated them. Over time, the Jews just kept quiet about their heritage, and those who did still believe in the Lord God of Israel, just kept it to themselves.

Ahasuerus was king of Persia at the time and history tells us, he wasn't much of a king.

That was the year Ahasuerus hosted a festival of feasts that lasted almost seven months! It was written about by his record keepers and historians of the day. He invited all the princes and powerful people from all over Persia. The purpose of this celebration was for one purpose: to show all **the riches of his glorious kingdom and the splendor of his excellent majesty.** (Esther 1:4)

Finally, the last, great, grand finale took place. All the riches of the kingdom were on display! Gold and silver, the finest of linen and purple that could be found. He even had a mosaic floor put in his grand garden; inlaid with alabaster, turquoise and black and white marble.

And for his finest display of ownership, he commanded his wife, Queen Vashti, to be brought, **wearing her royal crown, in order to show her beauty to the people and the officials, for she was beautiful to behold.** (Esther1:11)

Some historians tell us she was ordered to appear nude. Others say she was to dress in transparent veils. Either way, she was to display herself in order to show all these people one more, one-of-a-kind, costly thing the king owned.

But Queen Vashti refused to obey the king's command!

Ahasuerus was furious! He called his counselors together and asked, what does the law say we can do to her because she did not obey me, the king? We then find out, this was how he always conducted business. Evidently he never knew how to solve a problem or come up with an answer. Let someone else to it! (Esther 1:13) We'll see more of this.

The answer? Get rid of her!!! Have a beauty contest and pick a new queen to show off. And write a new law! All women will obey their husbands!

The king was pleased and did what he was told.

After he banished Vashti and signed the decree, he had second thoughts, but it was too late. Officers were sent through out the kingdom to bring back the most beautiful young virgins they could find.

Among those taken from their families, was Hadassah, Esther. She was an orphan who had been raised by her cousin Mordecai who raised her as if she were his own daughter. Now she was taken away to the kings citadel. For six months the young women were kept in seclusion and treated to a "beauty spa" Each one made an appearance before the king. And he loved Esther more than all the other virgins, so he set the royal crown upon her head and made her queen instead of Vashti.

Esther was Queen of Persia. But...Esther had a secret. She was a Jewess! Mordecai had told her to tell no one and she had not.

In those days and even today, some royals, some heads of state and some religious leaders, claimed they were deity on earth and therefore worthy of honor and homage (worship). They expected people to bow to them as they pass by.

So it was with Ahasuerus. He was given the position of deity and he could appoint others to that high estate. At this time he promoted a man named Haman to the second highest position in the land.

Now Mordecai was a business man and sat in the city gate every day with the other business men and city leaders. He also kept in contact with Esther every day, but no one knew he was a Jew, until......

The day Haman passed by the gate and people **bowed and paid homage to Haman, for so the king had commanded concerning him. But Mordecai would not bow or pay homage.** (Esther3:2)

This happened every day and Haman became angrier every day. Then he found out Mordecai was a Jew! Rather than punishing just Mordecai, he hatched a plan to destroy him and all the Jews in the kingdom!

Esther and Ahasuerus had been married four years when Haman finally approached the king with a suggestion. He had it all planned out right to the day everything was to take place. "You write a decree that all Jews in your kingdom must be destroyed and I will give you the money to do it!" Haman was willing to spend over three billion dollars to be used as a bounty on Jews!

And the king replied "do what you want and here is my ring, Use it to sign your papers in my name."

He didn't know he had just put a bounty on his own wife!

Letters of instructions were sent and the law issued to every province of the kingdom. And then published for all the Persians to read, even the date of the executions! **So the people should be ready for that day.** Instructions **to destroy, to kill, and to annihilate all the Jews, both young and old, little children and women, in one day, on the sixteenth day of the twelfth month** (Esther 3:13-14)and...... the Persians were to steal all their possessions.

All the Jews went into mourning. Mordecai and all the people went out into the city street wailing and crying, fasting and laying in sackcloth and ashes.

When word came to Queen Esther through her maids that Mordecai was in mourning, she had no idea why so she sent clothes for Mordecai so he would take off his sackcloth and stop mourning, but he would not accept them. When she sent another servant to find out what happened to cause his mourning, Mordecai gave the servant a copy of the decree to show Esther along with request. He asked her to go to the king and plead with him for her people.

Esther send the servant back to Mordecai, saying everyone knows; no one, not even me, can approach the king with out being summoned! The penalty is death! And I haven't been called to see the king in thirty days!

Mordecai sent back to her. **"Do not think in your heart that you will escape in the king's palace any more than all the other Jews. For if you remain completely silent at this time, relief and deliverance will arise for the Jews from another place but you and your father's house will perish. Yet who knows whether you have come to the kingdom for such a time as this?"** Esther answered **"Gather the Jews in the city. Fast for me three days. My maids and I will do the same. Then I will go to the king, which is against the law; and if I perish, I perish!"** (Esther 4:13-16)

At the end of three days, Esther put on her royal robes. She did not approach the king, but stood in the inner court of the kings palace. When the king saw her, he sent for her. He not only received her but offered her anything she wanted! All she asked, was for him and Haman to come to a dinner she had prepared. Instantly, the king sent for Haman and they went to her palace. After dinner the king again offered her anything she wanted and she replied, both of you come again tomorrow for a banquet and I will tell you want I want.

Haman left her palace so excited! He gathered all his family and friends and bragged on the invitation extended to him! "But even this doesn't make me happy as long a Mordecai is still alive." So his family told him to have a gallows prepared and hang Mordecai, then go enjoy the banquet! (Esther 5)

But, as he was overseeing the building of the gallows, the king sent for Haman, for some advice. The king wanted to honor a man and wanted to know the best way to do it.

Haman was overjoyed! How best for the king to honor "me"? he thought! Haman told the king to dress the man in one of the kings robes, put him on one of the kings horses with a royal crest for all to see and parade him through the city and then be brought to you, for you to bestow the honor.

What a day! His enemy would hang in a few minutes and he, Haman, himself, would have a great tribute from the king!

Then the king said, hurry! Do just what you have said! Do it for Mordecai! I just found out he saved my life a few months ago! Wwaaat? Mordecai? He had no choice but to arrange for the honor to be given to Mordecai that day.

That evening the king and Haman went to the banquet, (Esther7) and again the king offered Esther anything she wanted. And her answer was: **If it pleases the king, let my life be given me at my petition, and my people at my request. For we have been sold, my people and I, to be destroyed, to be killed and to be annihilated."** (Esther 7:3-4)

Ahasuerus didn't put two and two together! Who would dare to do such a thing, he demanded!

Esther replied: Haman!

Haman was hung that very hour on the gallows he had prepared for Mordecai.

Esther told the king how she and Mordecai were related and the king sent for Mordecai, presented him with the king's own signet ring. And appointed him over the house of Haman.

The king still did not understand what Esther had said. She had told him, she and Mordecai were Jews! The Jews were to be annihilated by the kings own proclamation! He just didn't get it!

Now Esther again spoke to the king. She fell at his feet, crying. Please do something about the execution date set for me and my people!

His reply? You take care of it! Do whatever it is you please. Here is my ring, use it to seal the orders and it will be done as you say. (Esther 8:8)

What he had already signed could not be changed, but, the new letter and decree permitted all the Jews in every city to join together and defend themselves and their property.

The appointed day arrived. All those who hated Jews were armed and prepared to help the king's men to destroy all the Jews and take their property. **The opposite occurred, in that the Jews themselves overpowered those who hated them........... And no one could withstand them because fear of them fell upon all the people**. (Esther 9:1-2) More than eighty thousand Persians died in two days. But none of their property or belongings were touched! This had to show the people the difference between themselves and God's people.

King Ahasuerus gave Haman's place of honor to Mordecai and he used it, to bring peace among all the people.

Esther and her uncle then instituted a national holiday for all the Jews in the kingdom to keep every year. A day of feasting and gift giving. A day to remember how God helped them defeat their enemies. They called it the days of Purim. (Esther 9:20-32)

Does Esther have a message for us?

You never know when God will need you! Always be ready! God will open a door for you, and if you choose not to go through it, He will open it for someone else. And they will receive the reward!

When I came to Troas to preach Christ's gospel, a door was opened to me by the Lord. (2 Corthian2:12)

FOOD FOR THOUGHT

1. The Lord, God of Israel is never mentioned in the Book of Esther, but do you see evidence of His hand in the events?
    Esther being chosen?
    The kings lack of interest in the laws and the ruling of his kingdom?
    The fear that came upon the Persians?
    Other events?

2. Do you see evidence of faith in her story? Whose? How was faith displayed? How is your faith displayed?
    The book of James

3. When did the Lord last open a door for you? Were you expecting it? Some one coming to you, asking you to pray with her? Did you see someone on the street or a parking lot that could have used your help? What was it He wanted you to do? Feed a hungry person? Take a sister to a doctor's appointment? Volunteer when the church needs help with a ministry? Do something for a neighbor? Answer someone's question about your faith?

    What excuses do we use when we refuse to go through a door the Lord opens for us?

4. If we refuse to go through the door because we are just too busy, or we don't know what to do or how we can help. Or we think, "I'll just let someone else will do it". What happens?

Esther 4:14   James 4:17

SONG   **LIVING BY FAITH**

CHAPTER TWENTY

ELIZABETH

Luke chapter1

About four hundred and fifty years have passed since the time of Esther and the last prophet sent by God was Malachi shorty after Esther's time. God had not sent a message to his people for four hundred years; not by prophets, or by angels or in dreams. During those years, a lot of the Jews who were taken into captivity chose to go back home to Judea. Some went to Jerusalem, the city where their temple was located, and over the years the city had grown to about forty thousand people. But during the Jewish festival times, it would grow to three times that or more!

Herod was king of Judea, appointed by Rome, and Rome ruled with an iron fist! Rome gave the Jews freedom to worship God and live by their religious law, but the leaders of the two Jewish sects could not agree on a lot things and they were causing division among the people. And to make matters worse, there was a constant rumor of a Messiah coming to lead the Jews in a revolt against Rome. Roman officials were constantly on alert for the smallest infraction, for the Romans hated the Jews anyway. Foolish people, worshiping only one god and could not even agree on how to do that! They were so divided among themselves and fighting for predominance, they needed to all be finished!

This is where we meet a woman named Elizabeth. She was married to Zacharias who was a priest of God. **And they were both righteous before God, walking in all the commandments and ordinances of the Lord blameless.** (Luke 1:5) He had been a priest for many years and now they were "senior citizens". Her husbands duties as priest called him away from home on a regular schedule to serve in the temple of the Lord. He would be away several days and she would be the keeper at home.

This time was no different. Elizabeth kissed her husband goodby and wished him safe journey to Jerusalem, as she always did.

But this time!! When he came home, their life was changed forever! Life would never be the same. To begin with Zacharias was mute! Could not say a word! And the story he told was incredible! He didn't tell her; he wrote it down.

While he was in the temple an angel from God came and spoke to him! With a message that was unbelievable! He and Elizabeth were going to have a baby boy! At their age! They were to name the baby John and he would be no ordinary man! He would be dedicated to God from conception with a Nazirite vow, just like the prophet Samuel. (Judges 13:5-7) Baby John **would be filled with the Holy Spirit from his mother's womb.** (Luke 1:11-17) AND he would be the one to prepare the way for the Savior of the world! The long waited-for Messiah!

And because Zacharias doubted the possibility, he was struck mute until the birth of his son.

Elizabeth was filled with joy! Finally, a son! A son of her own! Happiness! (Remember what we learned in the study of Rachel, about the shame of having no children)

When Elizabeth was six months pregnant, a young relative came for a visit. As soon as Elizabeth saw Mary come up to the house, baby John leaped in her womb and Elizabeth was filled with the Holy Spirit and she knew!! **Why is this granted to me, that the mother of my Lord should come to me!** (Luke 1:43) She knew Mary's baby was the Messiah they had been waiting for!

Mary's visit lasted about three months and she went back home. About three months later Elizabeth had her son and her husband could speak again! Her son grew to be a man of the wilderness; he had a mane of uncut hair and his clothes were made of animal skins. He was known as John the baptist (baptizer).

We don't hear of Elizabeth anymore but she leaves us a message.

God has a work prepared for each of us! Do not doubt God, if you are His child, He has a work for you!

When Paul wrote to the Christians in Ephesus, he told them (and us) when we be became Christians, **we were created in Christ Jesus for good works, which God prepared beforehand that we should walk in them.** (Ephesians 2:10)

FOOD FOR THOUGHT

1. God doesn't speak to us through angels today, but though His holy word. But, do you ever, like Zacharias, doubt what God tells you? Some people read a scripture and say "That can't be true." "God would never say that or do that!" "Did God really say that?"

    Psalm 119:160   2 Timothy 3:16   2 Peter 1:20-21

    Romans 15:4   1 John 5:13

2. Go back and read Luke 1:6. How did Elizabeth and her husband live their lives?

3. What can knowing and living by the words of God and His Son bring to our lives?

    Galatians 5:16-26

4. Be like Elizabeth! When you here the good news. When you see it come to life, Be Happy!!

    Luke 2:10   James 1:17   Romans 12:12,15

SONG   **SING AND BE HAPPY**

CHAPTER TWENTY-ONE

HERODIAS

Matthew 14:1-12   Mark 6:14-29

When we meet Herodias, she is married to Herod, the king of Judea. This Herod is the son of the Herod who had all the babies around Bethlehem murdered just thirty years before. Herodias and her husband had been receiving reports about a man preaching outside the city. The problem was, he was meddling in politics, saying a new kingdom was coming! The Jews were ready to kill him and there were other people calling this man a prophet of God! The God of the Jews had not sent a prophet for four hundred years! Now this! Herod had all he could do just to keep a semblance of order to appease Rome.

Then John told Herod something that changed everything! **"It is not lawful for you to have your brother's wife."** (Mark 6:18)

John was talking about Herodias. When Herodias heard this it made her so mad she wanted to kill John! How dare he publicly accuse her of such a thing! (even if it was true!)

She had left her first husband, Phillip to be with Herod. But... Phillip was her father's brother! And Herod was Phillip's half brother!

What a mess! And all this was against the law! By law, she should have never been married to either of these men! This so-called marriage was illegal, a public scandal; an open disregard of law, of God, and morality!

Mark tells us Herod feared John, knowing he was a righteous and holy man, But she wanted John dead! This put Herod in a bad spot. What was he to do? Dare he move against John, a prophet of God, in order to appease his wife? If he could work up enough courage to have John killed, Herodias would be satisfied, but....he would have a rebellion on his hands because the people of Judea believed and accepted John as a prophet.

But Herodias was determined! So, Herod had John arrested and put in prison to protect him from Herodias, at the same time, hoping this would appease her, until he could figure out what to do.

But Herodias was not to be denied. She would find a way! She waited. **Then an opportune day came** (Mark 6:21) Her husband's birthday! Perfect! This would be a huge celebration. Everyone who was anyone would be there. Food, wine, entertainment. A gala evening!

Just as she planned; after an evening of too much food and wine, Herod was an easy mark! Herodias enlisted her daughter's help. She danced before the king and all his guests and she was the star of the evening! Tradition tells us, she danced the dance of the seven veils. A very sensual dance intended to arouse the men. And it worked!

Herod then did a really stupid thing! He told the girl she could have anything she wanted. It's yours! You know everyone who was sober enough to think was aghast! Then Herod made it worse; he took an oath and told her she could have anything up to half of his kingdom!

How drunk was this man? Anything! Half his kingdom! Wealth! Power!

This was just what Herodias had counted on. When the girl asked her mother what she should ask for, it was none of those things! The girl went back into the banquet hall, in front of all the dignitaries, high officials and guests, and she told Herod **"I want you to give me at once the head of John the Baptist on a platter."** (Mark 6:25)

Instantly, Herod sobered up and regretted his rash actions. But everyone had heard his oath. He could not make things worse by refusing to keep an oath. So, immediately John was executed and his head was presented to the girl, just as she had asked. And the girl gave it to her mother, Herodius. (Mark 6:21-26)

We never again hear of Herodius or her daughter after that birthday celebration. But, this is not the last we will hear of Herod.

Herodius was an adulteress and a murderess, she was vindictive and manipulative. We are never told she repented or was sorry in any way for any of this.

I don't think we want to hear a message form her. Instead, let's read again Proverbs 31 and Galatians 5:22-23 and listen to the messages from Solomon and Paul.

FOOD FOR THOUGHT

1. Why did Herodius hate John so much? Could it be, she knew he was right? There have been other cases of people being killed because they were witnesses of a wrong doing. That is why some people avoid their families, they know their lifestyle is wrong. That is why criminals avoid the police officers, they know they are wrong.

2. Are we ever guilty of doing things we know are wrong? What are we do about it?

                              Acts 22:16

3. What is the result of willfully continuing in that sin?

                          Hebrews 10:26-29

4. What should we be doing?

        Proverbs 28:13   Psalm 32:5   1 John 1:9

SONG   **PRAY ALL THE TIME**

CHAPTER TWENTY-TWO

MARY, MOTHER OF JESUS

Matthew Mark Luke John

O f all the women in the Bible, we all know the story of Mary the best. She was a Jewish girl, probably about sixteen years old, living with her family in the city of Nazareth. She had brothers and sisters and she was engaged to be married to a man named Joseph, the local carpenter. She had heard about a relative that an angel was to have spoken to, but it was not anywhere around where she lived. And that was the first time in four hundred years God had spoken to any one!

But one day, an angel spoke to her! (Luke 1:26) The angel Gabriel was sent to her with a message from God! An astounding message! He told Mary she was going to have a baby! How can that be? She was a virgin. She can't have a baby, she's not married. In her community that was punished by stoning!

Then Gabriel told her, her baby would be a son. The long awaited Messiah! The Savior of the world! The Son of God! Not by a man but by the Holy Spirit! Luke described her as troubled, then we see hesitancy then acceptance and, because of her faith we see obedience when Mary said, **"Behold the maidservant of the Lord! Let it be to me according to your word."** (Luke 1:38)

We are not told any of the conversations Mary had with her parents or with Joseph, but I can imagine!

We do not know how he found out, but when Joseph was told, his world was turned upside down! What a fantastic story! An angel! A baby! The Holy Spirit! Who would believe that?! He was a business man, if that got out, he might loose his customers! Gossip will fly! They will stone Mary! He finally decided to just put her quietly away, maybe no one would find out and she would be left alone. And he would just have to get along without her.

The next thing we know, Luke tells us, Mary left town in a hurry and went to visit her mother's relatives.

Matthew tells us, while Mary was gone, an angel appeared to Joseph and reassured him, Mary was telling the truth! Into their keeping, God was sending His Son! And **Joseph did as the angel of the Lord commanded him and took to him his wife.** (Matthew 1:24) Don't you know Mary was finally happy!!

Luke picks up the story in chapter two. Their marriage took place and toward the end of her pregnancy, Caesar Augustus sent out a decree that everyone would return to the place of their birth and be counted; a census. Mary and Joseph packed up and went to Bethlehem, his hometown. About ninety miles on foot and riding on a donkey; on the road a little over a week and when they got there, the town was full of people, the inns were full and her baby was due any day! An Inn keeper said they could stay in his barn. But, that was better than out in the open. And that was where her baby boy was born, in a stable. A beautiful, healthy baby boy, in spite of all the travail! Now what is Mary feeling? Thankful!

That same day, some shepherds came to the barn and told Mary and Joseph a remarkable story! While they were out with their sheep an angel appeared to them! The angel said the long awaited Christ, the

Messiah had finally come and He had been born in this barn! Then the sky was full of angels! You could not count them all! And they were singing and praising God!

And all those (including Mary) marveled at those things told them. No heavenly visitations for four hundred years and now so many!

But Mary kept all these things and pondered them in her heart. (Luke 2:19)

Eight days later when Mary and Joseph made the trip to Jerusalem to have baby Jesus circumcised, another surprise awaited. A man named Simon knew they were coming and he had been waiting on them. He knew Jesus had been born and he knew what the future held for this baby and His mother! And Joseph and His mother marveled at those things which were spoken of Him

Then there was a woman named Anna, a prophetess there in the temple and the moment she saw the baby Jesus, she knew! She knew who He was and began telling everyone!

Mary, Joseph and their baby returned to Bethlehem and two years later, Matthew picks up the story. Mary and Joseph had settled into a routine of life, work and family, when some very strange men came to their door. They had been traveling for two years and had come from the far East to see her little boy. These men knew the prophecy of Micah 5:2 had been fulfilled in the birth of her Son! The men fell down and worshiped the Child Jesus and then presented him with wonderful treasures.

Again, that same night, an angel of the Lord appeared to Joseph. This time the angel told him to take Mary and the baby to Egypt! Now! That night! **Go and stay there until I bring you word; for Herod will seek the young Child to destroy Him.** (Matthew 2:13)

It would be three years before Herod died and the family was told by an angel they could go home. But God warned Joseph in a dream that Harod's son was now on the throne, and they were not to go back to Judea. So instead of Bethlehem, they went into Galilee to Nazareth. Home, back to her family! Relief? Joy?

We don't hear any more about this family until about seven years later and Luke picks up the story.

Mary and her family went to Jerusalem every year for the feast of the Passover. The year Jesus was twelve years old He went with them. After all the celebration, after a day on the road, they discovered Jesus was no where to be found; not with family, not with friends, no where! so Mary and Joseph went back to Jerusalem. Finally, after three days, they found Him in the temple with the teachers and everyone who heard Him were astonished at His understanding and answers He gave to their questions. When Mary and Joseph saw Him, and heard Him they were too were amazed, but as a mother, Mary reprimanded her son. She and Joseph had been worried to death! Luke tells us she was amazed then anxious. And then she was confused when Jesus answered her **"Did you not know that I must be about My father's business?"** (Luke 2:47-50)

But they did not understand. At least two more times in the following years, Jesus would gently remind her, she is human and He is not. But, He always regarded her as His mother. (John 2:4, Matthew 12:26)

For the next eighteen years, Jesus was a carpenter just like Joseph and worked in his shop. At some point, Mary and Joseph had four more sons and at least two daughters before Joseph died and left Mary a widow. As the oldest son, any of the family still at home, became the responsibility of Jesus. They were a Jewish family just like any other Jewish family in Nazareth.

But when Jesus turned thirty years old, everything changed. He went to find His relative, John, who had been preaching in the wilderness around the Jordan river. Jesus asked John to baptize Him and when He came up out of the water, for the first time, a public announcement was made of who Jesus really is. And God made the proclamation! **"You are my beloved Son; in You I am well pleased."** (Luke 3:21-22)

Jesus went into the wilderness and Mary didn't see her son for forty days, and when He came back, He began His new vocation as minister.

For three years, Mary watched as her first born Son was misunderstood, mistreated, called deranged, a liar and worse! His own family **went out to lay hold of Him, for they said "He is out of His mind"** (Mark 3:21)

She watched as He was arrested and brought to trial, found guilty of blasphemy and sentenced to death! She watched as her Son was hung on a cross like a common criminal! She watched as, while on the cross, Jesus gave the her care into the hands of His cousin, John, a believer, rather than to Mary's other sons who were not believers. And she watched Him draw His last breath.

Then she watched as Joseph of Arimathea buried her Son.

Now describe Mary.

Three days later we see unbelievable joy when she saw her Son alive again! (Matthew 28:1-8) And the overwhelming happiness when her sons, James and Jude became believers and followers of their brother Jesus! (Acts1:12-14, 1Corinthians 15:7)

That is the last time we see Mary; in that upper room with her sons. But we know she went to live with John and history tells us John took his family and lived in Ephesus where he became an elder in the church.

After reading Mary's story, what do you think her message would be? She has been on the mountain tops of joy and into the depths of despair. She has been startled, confused, hesitant, troubled, obedient, amazed and excited. She has been full of fear, relief, hope and joy.

I think her message comes through loud and clear!

Love her Son! Believe in Him!

But these things are written that you may believe that Jesus is the Christ, the Son of God, and that believing, you may have life in His name. John 20:31

1. When was Mary In the valley?

2. Have you been in the valley of despair? Do we have assurance of help in these times?

       Psalm 16:1   Psalm 27:5-7   Psalm 46:1-11
      Proverbs 3:25-26 Philippians 4:6-9 2 Timothy 1:7,12
       Hebrews 10:35,36   Romans 12:12

3. When was Mary on the mountain top?
    Have you been on the mountain top? How did you react?

       Psalm 47:1-3   Psalm 92:4-5   Psalm118:24
      Psalms 126:2-3   Romans 14:17   Romans 15:13
       Philippians 4:4 1   Peter 1:8-9

SONG   I BELIEVE IN THE ONE THEY CALL JESUS

CHAPTER TWENTY-THREE

SALOME

Matthew, Mark, Luke, John, Acts1:3-14, 2:1-4

Salome is one of the puzzles in the Bible. Who was She? Open your Bibles with me to Matthew 27:56, Mark 15:40, John 19:25. Matthew names three women at the cross: the mother of Zebedees' sons, Mary Magdalene, and Mary mother of James and Joses.

Mark names three women at the cross: Salome, Mary Magdalene, Mary, mother of James the Less and Joses

Luke does not give the names of the women at the cross.

John names four women there: Jesus' mother and her sister, Mary wife of Clopas and Mary Magdalene.

Salome was the mother of Zebedees' sons and the sister of Mary. Zebedees' sons were James and John. Now that we know who she is, lets hear her story.

All the prophets, since Abraham had told the Children of Israel, (the Jews) that one day a Messiah would come! Three hundred fifty one recorded prophecies about Him; a deliverer, one who would destroy their enemies, a warrior, a ruler, the Christ, of the tribe of Judah. A King of Israel. And on and on. But not one prophecy said WHEN.

And they were still waiting. If ever their people needed a deliverer, it was now! The powers of Rome were growing all the time. Herod was just a puppet of Rome, and they needed the Messiah to come.

Then one day, Salome's sister came into the house with the most outlandish story. Mary claimed she was going to give birth to the long awaited Messiah! And she did! Her Son, Jesus, grew up to be a preacher and told the people He was the Messiah. He performed miracles, healed people and said things like no man ever before Him. Many people believed Him and He had a great following everywhere He went.

He, Jesus was their deliverer! Their Messiah! He would raise up an army and defeat Rome restore the Kingdom of Israel! Salome believed it. All of His disciples believed it. The twelve men He chose to be His apostles believed it.

None of them understood the kingdom Jesus spoke of was a spiritual kingdom.

When Jesus had chosen Salome's two sons to be His chosen apostles, she did not understand. Instead, she came to Jesus **asking something from Him, grant that these two sons of mine may sit, one on Your right hand and the other on the left, in your kingdom. You do not know what you ask Jesus answered.** (Matthew 20:20-28) She was asking for positions of power for her sons when Jesus would restore the Kingdom of Israel. He answered her and then went on to explain, His people will not exercise authority over others! His people will be servants to others!

Later, even at the time of Jesus' arrest and crucifixion, Salome and all the others did not understand the concept of a spiritual kingdom. Even when Jesus said **My kingdom is not of this world** (John 18:36) they did not understand.

Salome and all the others believed Jesus was the son of God, the Messiah.........but they were confused about His kingdom.

When Jesus died on the cross and was buried, His followers were not sure what had just happened! Salome was there with her sister and some others and along with the terrible sorrow, there were questions. What about the kingdom Jesus was to build? Who would build it now? With Jesus dead, what were they to do? Was the grand plan over? Were they to just forget it and go back to their lives where they left off three years ago?

Salome went with her sister and some other women on that following Sunday morning to anoint the body of Jesus and received the shock of their lives! Jesus was alive! He talked to them! He told them to go tell His apostles and others.

Later, Jesus appeared to His apostles and **when they saw Him, they worshiped Him, but some doubted.** (Matthew 28:17) A man named Cleopas left Jerusalem and he said "But we were hoping that it was He who was going to redeem Israel." (Luke 24:21) NKJV They all knew who He was, the Son of God, the Messiah, the Christ, but didn't understand just what that meant.

Luke tells us the rest of the story. (Acts 1:3-14)

For forty days Jesus was with His followers. The last time Jesus was with His followers, He told them, Do not go home! Stay here in Jerusalem and wait! Wait for the promise to be fulfilled. And again, His followers asked Him, Lord will you at this time restore the kingdom to Israel?

They still did not understand what the promised kingdom was to be, and as they stood watching, He was lifted up into the clouds out of their sight.

Then Luke tells us of a grand new beginning! Luke tells us His followers went back up into the upper room where they had been with Jesus so many times. Mary and her sons were there along with some other women. Was Salome there with her sister and her own sons?

Then comes the day when they all understand!

Luke tells us the same group of people were in that upper room when the Holy Spirit, the promised Comforter, the Helper, the one who would guide them into all truth and give them understanding, came to them!

Now Salome and all the others understand the meaning of the Kingdom of Christ! His church was born that day! A spiritual kingdom! A spiritual war! And Salome was there! That day, three thousand people were added to the kingdom (Acts 2:41)

We don't hear of Salome anymore, but we a lot about her two sons. James was killed by King Herod for preaching Jesus. (Acts 12:1-2) Her other son, John, spent the rest of his life spreading the gospel of Christ. He was put into excile for preaching Jesus, where he then recorded the last words of Christ! Christ's last message to His people! (Book of Revelation) When he was released, he returned to Ephesus. He was the only apostle to die a natural death of old age.

What would be Salome's message to us?

The kingdom of Christ, His church, was not brought to earth to defeat a ruthless government, but to defeat our sinful past! And to help us live the rest of our lives for Him!

Seek ye first the kingdom of God and His righteousness
(Matthew 6:33)

FOOD FOR THOUGHT

1. Do you or someone you know, like Salome, have questions or doubts about what the kingdom is?
   John3:1-7   Romans14:17   1Corinthians 6:9-11
   Ephesians 3:15-2   Colossians1:12-14   1Peter 2:9-10

2. When Christ comes back, what will happen to His kingdom?
   2Peter 1:11   1Corinthians 15:24

3. Are you part of His kingdom?
   John 3:1-7   Acts 2:38

SONG   **SEEK YE FIRST THE KINGDOM OF GOD**

MARY OF BETHANY

| Matthew 26 | Mark 14 |
| Luke 7 &10 | John 11&12 |

This Mary is the sister of Martha and Lazarus. This is another one of those occasions where we have to put the puzzle pieces together.

Lets begin with a dinner at the house of a Pharisee. This was not long after Jesus began His ministry. After the host and his guests were seated, an uninvited woman just shows up. **She brought an alabaster flask of fragrant oil and stood at His feet behind Him weeping; and she began to wash His feet with her tears and wiped them with the hair of her head; she kissed His feet and anointed them with the fragrant oil** (Luke 7-36-50) (This is the first time we see this woman.)

This was a heart broken woman. She spent her money for this oil and used her hair to wipe His feet. In the Jewish culture, a woman's hair was her crowing glory; something to be prized and cared for, and she used hers as a servant would use a towel!

The host thought to himself, this woman is a sinner. How did he know that? Did he know her? Jesus knew his thoughts and began teaching a lesson on forgiveness. At the end of His lesson, Jesus told the woman her sins were forgiven.

Now, lets skip ahead in our story and look at John 11:1-2 This is the account John wrote of the death of Lazarus. This happened in Bethany, the town of Mary and Martha, about two miles from Jerusalem. **It was that Mary who anointed the Lord with fragrant oil and wiped His feet with her hair whose brother Lazarus was sick.** (John 12:2) John makes it clear, that woman was Mary, the sister of Martha and Lazarus. And that was the first time we met her. What was her sin? We do not know. We are not told. John didn't bring it up, after all Jesus had forgiven her!

Now...A short time later, we see Mary the second time. Luke tells us Jesus is at the house of Martha and she has prepared a meal. Martha was busy being a good hostess, but her sister, Mary, was not helping, because she also sat at Jesus' feet and was listening to His word.

Even today, it is said, when a student is learning from a teacher, the student sits at the feet of the teacher. Paul sat at the feet of Gamaliel. There were not chairs, as we know them, but cushions on the floor and teachers stood in the middle of the room. Now teachers sit at the front of the room, sometimes up on a small dais and students sit lower (at his feet).

Can you imagine sitting at the feet of Jesus? Watching Him? Listening to Him?

When Martha complained to Jesus about Mary's lack of help, Jesus replied: **"Mary has chosen the good part, which will not be taken away from her."** (Luke10:42) What was He talking about? Matthew records Jesus saying; **"Heaven and earth shall pass away, but My words will by no means pass away."** (Matthew 24:35) The good part was His words, His teachings.

The third time we see Mary, her brother, Lazarus has died. (John 11:1-44)

When we read this, we see a woman who knows Jesus has healed many people and she knows Jesus can heal her brother, a man Jesus loved. She sent word to Jesus days before, but He didn't come. He was close by in Jerusalem, why didn't He come?

When Jesus finally arrived four days later, Lazarus had died. Mary ran to meet Him, "Lord If you had been here, my brother would not have died." She knew Jesus could have healed Lazarus. She knew it! But Jesus did not heal Lazarus, He raised him from the dead! Can you imagine her reaction when her brother walked out of that tomb?!

The fourth time we see Mary, it was six days before the Passover. (John 12:1-8) Again, in Bethany, at Martha's house.

Martha was serving supper prepared for Jesus and Lazarus and some of His disciples were also there. Again, Mary had taken on the role of a servant; on her knees, she anointed the feet of Jesus and wiped His feet with her hair. And again, Mary is criticized! First by the Pharisees, then Martha, and now by one of Jesus' disciples, Judas Iscariot. Why wasn't this oil sold (she had spent a year's salary on the oil she used that day!) and given to us to serve the poor? He was such a hypocrite! And a thief!

And again, Jesus defended Mary! **"Let her alone, she has kept this for the day of my burial. For the poor you have with you always, but Me you do not have always."** (John 12:7-8)

The last time we see Mary, it is just a few days before Jesus would be crucified. (Matthew 26:6-13; Mark 14:1-9) Jesus and His disciples are again in Bethany, at the house of Simon the leper. This man was no longer a leper, or he could not have been at home or even in town. He would have been an outcast of society.

NOTE: After a lot of research, many scholars believe this was the same man, the Pharisee who had invited Jesus to supper before. The man who knew who Mary was and called her a sinner. At some point, he had been stricken with leprosy and then healed. This time Mary is back in his house again and he does not object, which leads them to believe Simon's house and Martha's house may have been the same house and they may have been married. Had Jesus also healed Simon of his leprosy? We are never told. Neither are we told where Mary or her brother, Lazarus lived but they are in this house a lot. (could this another one of the puzzles we have talked about?)

This woman is so grateful for all Jesus has done; forgiving her, raising her brother from the dead, possibly healing her brother-in law, she again brings expensive oil but this time she doesn't anoint His feet, she anoints Jesus' head. And again, she is criticized! By Jesus' disciples. And once more, Jesus defends her. **"Assuredly I say to you, wherever this gospel is preached in the whole world, what this woman has done will also be told, as a memorial to her."** (Matthew 26:13, Mark 14:9)

That is the last time we see Mary of Bethany. But people have been reading her story and seeing her faith for almost two thousand years!

What would be her message to us? I think it is two fold.

First..... Put Jesus first! Make time for Him! Listen to Him.
Thy word is a lamp unto my feet (Psalms 119:105)
Second......Be grateful to Jesus!
Enter into His gates with thanksgiving, And into His courts with praise. Be thankful to Him and bless His name.
(Psalm 100:4)

FOOD FOR THOUGHT

1. Do you spend time listening to Jesus?
   John 16:6   Acts 17:11   Romans 15:4

2. Will Jesus defend us?
   Matthew 10:33   1 Timothy 2:5   1 John 2:1

3. Are you thankful for what Jesus and His Father do for you? Do you tell Them or do you take it for granted they know you are thankful.
   Isaiah 12:4-52   Ephesians 5:19-20
   Colossians 3:15-17   1 Thessalonians 5:16-18
   Hebrews 13:15

**2 SONGS   I WILL ENTER HIS GATE
THANK YOU LORD FOR LOVING ME**

CHAPTER TWENTY-FIVE

MARY MAGDALENE

Matthew 27:55-61   Mark 15:40-41, 16:1-8
Luke 8:2, 23:55   John 20:11-18

We are told very little about Mary Magdalene, but what a story she can tell us! Her name tells us she came from the region of Magdala, about a hundred and fourteen miles from Jerusalem.

The first time we see her name, she is listed among several women, Jesus healed of evil spirits (demons) and infirmities. Mary Magdalene was released from seven devils. (Luke 8:2-3)

We are not told what these demons were or what the manifestations were. But, for some reason, a lot of people think these women, in particular, Mary Magdalene, were prostitutes. Scripture does not tell us that. It isn't even hinted at.

Matthew listed demon possession in a list of illnesses (Matthew 4:34) Many Bible scholars believe it was mental illness, or anything medical science did not understand and had no answer for at the time.

There was a man brought to Jesus who was demon possessed and he was blind and mute. (Matthew 2:22)

Demons sometimes caused people to act irrationality, aggressively or in a frighting way. (Matthew 8:28-32 Mark 9:17-22)

There was one time Jesus cast demons into a herd of swine, (Matthew 8:28-32) That is the only time we read of demons in anything other than human beings. Scripture never tells us demons inhabited an inanimate object, such as a dwelling, a place of business or a conveyance.

No scripture tells us demons or evil spirits caused people to live a sinful life. Some of the Jews in the Bible seemed to think these things were a sign of someones sin because they had no other explanation. Sin has always been a choice! Ever since Adam and Eve.

Scripture tells us Jesus said these things happened to show the power of God. To prove He was the Son of God. (John 9:3-4, Matthew 12:28)

And that is what happened to Mary Magdalene and the other women. She was healed to show the power of God. And the result was, these women became followers of Jesus! They helped support His ministry with their own money and they accompanied Him on His journey.

The next time we see Mary Magdalene was on a Friday morning. She was at the feet of the cross on which Jesus was hanging and she was there grieving with His mother.

Her Healer, her Teacher was gone! Hope for His Kingdom was gone! Faith was damaged! Who were they supposed to turn to now? There never was one like Him!

And then we see Mary Magdalene grieving in the garden when Nicodemus buried her best Friend.

We see her again two days later. Mark tells us **Now when He arose early on the first day of the week, He appeared first to Mary Magdalene out of whom He had cast seven devils** (Mark 16:9)

John tells us the details of that first appearance. (John 20:11-18) We see Mary Magdalene standing, weeping at the tomb and she stooped down and looked inside one more time and this time there were two angels! They asked Mary why she was crying and she she said someone took her Lord away and she didn't know where they took Him. She turned to leave and saw who she thought was the gardener. She asked the man to tell her where he had taken Jesus so she could go get His body. When the man replied by saying her name, she immediately knew who He was! Jesus!

Everything changed! Her Teacher! Her Healer! The One who restored her was here! Alive! Evidently she ran toward Him to embrace Him, for He said **"Do not cling to Me for I have not yet ascended to My Father and your Father; but go to My brethren and say to them, I am ascending to My Father and to my God and to your God."** (John 20:17)

Hope restored! Faith renewed! Her Father! Her God!

We never see her name in scripture again, but we can be sure she was among the women with Mary the mother of Jesus and His brothers in that upper room in Jerusalem, that day when the long awaited for kingdom was established on the earth. (Acts 1:14)

If Mary Magdalene could speak to us today, what would her message be?

Always look for Jesus! Stay with Him! Follow Him!

Looking unto Jesus, the author and finisher of our faith.
(Hebrews 12:2)

FOOD FOR THOUGHT

1. Do you, Like Mary Magdalene, walk with Jesus through your day or do you leave Him behind until a more convenient time? When is that?

    Psalm 6:28   Psalm 119:105   1 Chronicles16:11-12

    Matthew 6:33   Ephesians 5:15-17

    One of the saddest passages in the Bible is Acts 26:27-28

2. Are the words: church, Jesus, worship, Father, prayer, blessings among the words of your daily vocabulary? Or only when you are with "church people"?

    Deuteronomy 6:6-9

3. Do you speak with God on and off through your day, or like so many folks, only at meal time? Do you take time to thank Him for everything? Every blessing, as it happens or as you see it!

    1 Thessalonians 5:17-18

SONG   HE LIVES

CHAPTER TWENTY-SIX

JOANNA

Luke 8:1-3   Luke 23:55   Luke 24:10

We are told Joanna was married to Chuza, the house steward of King Herod. He managed Herod's staff and he was the purchasing agent and bill payer for Herod. He was a man of much responsibility and influence. He and his wife Joanna lived on the place grounds and were known by all of society, but Joanna was different from the other women who moved in such circles. Maybe it was her illness or disease that set her apart. Or maybe, it was her longing for something different.

The first time we meet Joanna, she and Mary Magdalene and the other women, had been healed by Jesus. We are not told what any of them suffered with, only that Jesus healed them and they became His followers and supported His work.

Joanna, was at the crucifixion of Jesus along with other women who also ministered to Him. She was there at His burial and Luke tells us she was one of the women who came to the tomb early on the first day of the week when the earthquake happened! She saw the angel! And she saw the risen Savior! He spoke to her and the other women! Was she also among the women in the upper room on Pentecost?

About thirty years later, Luke wrote an epistle to his friend, Theopilus and told him about a man named Manaen. (Acts 13:1) Manaen and Herod the were step brothers and had been raised together. Herod was the one who had James the brother of John beheaded. And, Luke said Manaen was a member of the church in Antioch!

I wonder how Manaen heard about Jesus? You know he didn't hear good things about Jesus from Herod! I wonder if Joanna had anything to do with telling Manaen about her Healer and Teacher; the One who was resurrected from the dead and who established a new kingdom?

We don't heard any more about Joanna, but for the almost two thousand years people have been reading her story.

She gave of her time and her money. She showed her love, her gratefulness and her faith and she told others about Jesus, all for the glory of her Savior.

What would be her message to us?

Tell everyone you know about Jesus and what He did for you!

"I believed and therefore I spoke" (2 Corinthians 4:13)

FOOD FOR THOUGHT

1. What did Jesus do for Joanna?
   What has Jesus done for you?

2. What did Joanna do in return?

3. Are we tell others what Jesus did for us?
   Mark 16:15 -16   1 Peter 3:15
   2Corinthians 4:13-15

SONG   **RING OUT THE MESSAGE**

CHAPTER TWENTY-SEVEN

MARTHA

Luke 10:38-42   John 11:1-28
John12:1-8

Martha welcomed Him into her house. And she had a sister called Mary, who also sat at Jesus feet and heard His word (Luke 10:38)

Jesus and His disciples were in Martha's house many times, for meals, for rest and fellowship and for times of learning. Martha's sister, Mary was also listening to Jesus, but Luke says Martha was distracted.

This time she and her household had prepared a meal for her guests and it was time to serve, so she got up and went into the other room and was getting things ready and Jesus was still teaching.

It was time to get dinner on the table and her sister was still in the other room listening to Jesus, instead of helping. When Mary still didn't get up to help, Martha went back and complained to Jesus, **"Lord, do you not care that my sister has left me to serve alone? Therefore, tell her to help me."** (Luke 10:40)

We can sit here and find fault and accuse Martha, but would we have been different? Remember, no canned or frozen foods, no refrigerators or microwaves, no boxed cake mixes. Meat was freshly killed that day. Talk about cooking from scratch! Mary and the servants probably helped her get everything ready, but Mary wasn't helping her serve! How many people? Was her brother, Lazarus there? Probably. How many of the disciples were with Him? They went every place He did. Were there others there also to hear Jesus speak?

Then Jesus rebuked her. Corrected her!

Did He find fault with her for being a hard worker? A good hostess? What did she do wrong? She sounds like the woman in Proverbs!

Preparing a meal and serving it was not wrong, but she allowed herself to become so worried and agitated that she got upset and interrupted the lesson for everyone else! She tried to shame Mary and she was disrespectful to everyone in the room, including Jesus! Sounds like she is finding fault with Him! Why don't You do something?! She was telling Him what to do! But, Remember, Jesus was close friends with this family and she was probably used to giving orders and running her house.

Jesus answered her and said to her, **Martha, Martha, you are worried and troubled about many things. But one thing is needed, and Mary has chosen that good part, which will not be taken away.** (Luke 10:41-42)

Don't worry about physical things. Take care of business, do your work and take care of others, BUT do not let these things upset you. Don't get all out of sorts, say hurtful things and be disrespectful. Just do your job and don't worry about what someone else is doing. You do what you can, just take care of your attitude! So what if dinner was a little late?

It used to be that preachers would keep our mothers on Sundays and preach for an hour, and then the women would go home and fix dinner for their family plus company from church, sometimes the preacher's family. But now preachers are limited to about twenty minutes, so everyone can get out and get to the restaurant! How long would we postpone dinner to listen to the voice of Jesus?

Now lets turn our Bibles over to the book of John and see Martha for the second time.

Martha's brother, Lazarus has died. She knew Jesus had healed other sick people, so she and Mary had sent for Him several days ago to come and heal Lazarus. Jesus was in Jerusalem at the time, just as few miles down the road, but He didn't come and now it was too late, Lazarus had died three days ago.

When she heard Jesus was finally coming, she ran down the road to meet Him. **Lord if you had been here, my brother would not have died! even now I know that whatever You Ask of God, God will give You.** (John 11:21-22) She had faith in her Lord and her friend, that He could somehow heal Lazarus. But when Jesus told her, her brother would rise again she misunderstood! She believed in the resurrection. The day we all will rise from the grave, but what about Lazarus? Today? Jesus replied, **And whoever believes in Me shall never die. Do you believe this? And she said to Him**, **Yes, Lord, I believe You are the Christ, the Son of God who is come into the world** (John 11:26-27)

When she said that, we again see her faith! But she still wanted Lazarus back today, not later on the day of resurrection. she went back to the house to find her sister and tell her, Jesus was here.

Jesus was moved to tears in sympathy for these two sisters and knowing His friend suffered and died of his sickness. He asked to be taken to the tomb were her brother was laid. When He told someone to take the stone away from the door of the tomb, Martha told Him Lazarus had been dead four days and his body was decaying. Now is not the time to open a tomb, the smell would be terrible and you would not want to look at the body!

Jesus asked, **Did I not say to you that if you would believe you would see the glory of God?** (John 11:40)

We are not told her reaction when she saw her brother walk out of that tomb; when she saw him freed from the grave clothes and walking toward Jesus and his family.

The third time we see Martha, it is just as few days before Jesus would be crucified and she has again prepared a meal for Jesus and His disciples and her brother Lazarus. (John 12:1-8) Mary is also there. But this time there is no problem. Maybe Mary has learned to be a little more helpful, or Martha has learned to be a little more understanding and patient. Either way, this time, Martha looks even more like the woman described in Proverbs.

We never hear of Martha again, but knowing her as we do, you know she served many more suppers in her house, for family and friends. Possibly even some the disciples from time to time. I wonder, if when she was preparing and serving those meals, if she remembered serving Jesus and thought, If Jesus could raise my brother from the dead, He could have put supper on the table anytime He was ready! I was anxious about nothing!

What would Martha's message be for us?

You serve Jesus and His followers the very best way you can!

Not lacking in diligence, fervent in spirit, serving the Lord

(Romans 12:11)

FOOD FOR THOUGHT

1. 1. Does the Lord, Himself, today, sitting on the right hand of God, need me to feed Him, clothe Him, provide for Him?
   How do I serve Him today?

   Matthew 25:35-46

2. Do you criticize others for they way they serve?

   Galatians 6:4-5

3. Does everyone need to do the same work? Or do it the same way, to be pleasing to the Lord?

   1Corinthians 12:20-27

SONG **TO THE WORK**

CHAPTER TWENTY-EIGHT

THE WOMAN OF PHOENICIA

Matthew 15:21-28   Mark 7:24-30

I f you back up and start at the end of Matthew chapter four, you will see the traveling, teaching and healing Jesus had been doing. He was a man, just like us; you know He had to be tired. Every time He healed someone, that took strength from Him. Every where He went, He walked all over Judea, Galilee and Sameria. Constantly teaching and defending His authority. Every once in a while He went off by Himself to pray and be alone and now Jesus and His disciples went back to the region of Tyre and Sidon. These two cities were located in Phoenicia. Mark tells us He went to a house and didn't want anyone to know He was there.

But someone found out He was there.

She was a woman who lived somewhere in Phoenicia and she was not a Jew, but Greek. She had heard about Jesus and knew He was a Jew, and a descendant of King David. She knew how Jews felt about her people. They were the chosen people of their God, her people were not. But she had also heard of the healings He had conducted. She heard about Him healing the mother-law of one of his disciples. He had healed a paralytic. Everyone heard about Him healing the two demon-possessed men! He even cured a leper! He had even cured some of her own countrymen! (Luke 6:17-18) If Jesus could cure all those people, He could cure her daughter of an unclean spirit, if He was willing.

She knew the Jews considered her people dogs, but if this Man could cure her daughter, she could stand the abuse. So, she went to the house where He was staying and cried out to Him. Mark tells us she fell at His feet. And she kept asking Him to cast the demon out of her daughter.(Mark 7:25-26) **Have mercy on me, O Lord, son of David! My daughter is severely demon possessed.** (Matthew 15:22)

There was just one problem...Jesus was sent by His Father **to go to lost sheep of Israel** (Matthew10:5) Not to the Gentiles. Not yet, in time, but not yet.

The Jews, including His disciples would need more teaching to understand that Jesus came to fulfill a promise God made to Abraham over twenty one hundred years before: **And in your seed all the family of the earth will be blessed.** (Genesis 12:3) Jesus was to bring salvation **to the Jews first and then the Greek.** (Romans 1:16). But that was a hard concept for the Jews to accept. For all these years they have been the "people of God". They would learn that one day all people would be recognized as the children of God. But they were not there yet.

When Jesus tried to explain this to her, **she came and worshiped Him saying Lord help me!** (Matthew 15:25)

Jesus replied: **Let the children be filled first, for it is not good to take the children's bread and throw it to the little dogs.** (Mark 7:27) And she answered and said **Yes Lord, yet even little dogs under the table eat from the children's crumbs.**(Mark 7:28)

Jesus saw her great faith and granted her petition!

When she arrived at her home, she found her daughter had been completely cured the very hour Jesus said the words!

That is the last we hear of this woman, but her story has been told for almost two thousand years. God inspired men wrote this and it has been preserved for us for a reason.

What is her message to us, today?

Jesus is for everyone! Jew and Gentile! We are all His children, His family!

Go into all the world (all nations) **and preach the gospel to every creature.** (Mark 16:15)

FOOD FOR THOUGHT

1. Are there people today, willing to go against their culture, their people, to seek out Jesus? Do you know someone who was removed from their family because they became a follower of Jesus? How great was their faith?

2. Do you love your children enough to step out on faith and approach Jesus for them? Or take them to Jesus? Even if your people did not approve?

    1Samuel1:27-28   Proverbs 20:11   Isaiah 54:13
                          Matthew 10:14

3. Is there ever a time when Jesus is not accessible to you? Do you, like the woman from Phoenicia need to go to a particular place to find Jesus; a church building, an altar, or a special room? Is He only available at certain places, at special times?

    1 Thessalonians 5:17   Ephesians 6:18
                Hebrews 13:5-6

SONG   **PRAY ALL THE TIME**

CHAPTER TWENTY-NINE

THE POOR WIDOW

Luke 21:1-4

ack up to the last few verses of the last chapter. What had Jesus just said? **Beware of the scribes** (Luke 20:46) Who were the scribes? They were lawyers and they were the authority on what the Law of Moses said and what it meant. By the first century, the Sanhedrin court, the priests and the scribes had added to, and in some cases, found loopholes and made ways to go around the law or change the meaning. Under the Law given to Moses, the widows, the fatherless and the homeless were to be protected. Now...not so much.

Why did Jesus say beware of the scribes? They were self important and they stole widows houses under pretense of serving God. Just as He was talking about this, He looked and saw people putting their offerings in the plate at the temple.

Then He looked up and saw the rich putting their gifts into the treasury and He saw a certain poor widow putting in her two mites.

So He said, Truly I say to you that this poor widow has put in more than all; for these out of their abundance have put in offerings

for God, but she out of her poverty has put in all the livelihood that she had. (Luke 21:1-4)

There was always a priest standing by the money box, seeing what the people were giving. The Law required ten percent of what you had. As a faithful Jew this woman was expected to give, and she did. She gave all she could; all she had. What would have been ten percent of two mites? She gave it all!

Instead of helping this poor widow, those in power were more than willing to accept all she had. She gave all she could. Why would she do that? What kind of heart did she have? A selfish heart? A loving, merciful heart? She was trying to serve God as best she could.

Today, under the New Covenant, the Law of Christ, we are not required to give a specific amount. So what is too little and what is enough? Open your Bible and read 1Corinthians 8 & 9. read it again, Paul said: think about it, pray about it, plan ahead, give all you can, but do it willingly and cheerfully!

But, remember, your money is not most important thing you give to God!

One of the most misused passages in the New Testament is Luke 6:38. Open you Bibles with me, and read Luke 6:27-35. Jesus was telling His listeners how to treat other people, even your enemies. How to love all people. How to show mercy to them. How? give them money or your clothes, even lend to them, hoping for nothing in return; and we will be the children of the highest! Children of God! That is our reward!

Now, read Luke 6:36-37 Give mercy, by loving your enemies! Forgiving them! Showing mercy to them! Don't be too quick to judge; you don't always know their circumstances.

Jesus said to LOVE people, GIVE to people. Give mercy to everyone by helping and giving to them. Not by judging them, but forgiving them. Friends and enemies alike. Clothes, food, money, forgiveness. And expect nothing in return!!! That is what mercy is.

Now read the next verse. **Give, and it will be given to you: Good measure, pressed down shaken together and running over will be**

put into your bosom(your heart).(Luke 6:38) Into your heart! Not into your wallet! Jesus did not say....give all the money you can and God will make you rich! He said.... FREELY GIVE forgiveness and mercy in any way and in every way you can, and God will will give even more forgiveness and mercy to you! Give and it will be given back to you, more than you will ever have to give have the capability to give!

What would this poor widow say to us today?

Look into your heart, be honest with God and give everything you can to the Lord.

Blessed are the merciful for they shall obtain mercy.
(Matthew 5:7)

FOOD FOR THOUGHT

1. Be like the widow, Do all you can, expecting nothing in return.
   Acts 20:35   2 Corinthians 8:10-15   2 Corinthians 9:6-15

2. Was God ever satisfied with "second best" or something "left over"?
   Leviticus 22:19-20   Malachi 1:11-14

3. In addition to your money, what can you give to the Lord?
   Luke 6:27-38

4. Make a list of how you can show mercy today.

SONG   GIVE OF YOUR BEST TO THE MASTER

CHAPTER THIRTY

THE WOMAN AT THE WELL

John 4:1-42

There was a well near the city of Sychar of Samaria. It had been dug two thousand years before by Jacob, the grandson of Abraham. And women had been watering their flocks and drawing water for their homes ever since. This was a daily chore to be done early, before the heat of the day. There was a woman who waited until the others had left. It was noon when she came to draw her water.

When she arrived, there was a man sitting there and He asked her for a drink. He should never have spoken to her. A woman by herself! And He wasn't even a Samaritan, He was a Jew! Jews didn't have anything to do with Samaritans. "Why are you asking me for a drink?" she asked.

The Man replied "**If you knew who it is who says to you, 'Give Me a drink', you would have asked Him, and He would have given you living water.**" (John 4:10)

She didn't understand. He didn't have a bucket to draw water to give her. So where was He going to get that living water? What was living water?

All water gave life to the thirsty. Jacob had given them this well and it was a deep well with good water. Where was He going to get better water?

He answered her, "**whoever drinks of the water that I shall give him will never thirst. But the water I give him will become in him a fountain of water springing up into everlasting life.**" (John 4:14)

What was He telling her? Can you imagine her surprise? If she drinks of this Man's water, she will never be thirsty again! Never need to draw water again! She was thinking of wet water to quench physical thirst. Of course she asked Him to give her some of His water!

But He suddenly changed the subject and the conversation got really odd! He told her to go get her husband, and when she told Him, she did not have a husband, He said I know you don't, you have had five and you are not married to the man you are living with. How did He know? He must have been a prophet.

And then she changed the subject! For generations, we Samaritans have worshiped the Lord God, just as you Jews do, but we have worshiped on Mount Gerizim (Judges 9:6-7) and you Jews say Jerusalem is the only place to go to worship.

Jesus replied, "**believe Me, the hour is coming when you will neither on this mountain nor in Jerusalem worship the Father.**" (John 4:21)

She had been taught just like all Jews had, that one day the Messiah would come and explain all things. But they had been waiting for so long! Fifteen hundred years, was this possible?

And then the biggest surprise of her life! "**I who speak to you am He.**" (John 4:26)

She didn't even take time to gather her belongings, she ran back to the city, not to her home, but to the men, probably those sitting in the gate conducting business, and told them to come and see a man who knew all about her.

Because she went back and told the others that she thought she may have found the Christ, many of them went to the well and urged Him to stay and talk to them also. He stayed two days and in that time many more became believers.

During those two days, do you think Jesus explained the things He had said to the woman?

Did He explain the Living water? Did He quote the prophet, Jeremiah? God told Jeremiah **"My people have forsaken Me, the Fountain of Living Waters"** (Jeremiah 2:13)

Isaiah wrote, **"With joy you will draw water from the wells of salvation"** (Isaiah12:3)

What is the Living Water? The very words of God! John wrote, by inspiration of the Holy Spirit, that Jesus is the Word of God come to earth in the flesh.(John 1:1-5) Now Jesus said, He is the living water, one and the same. The words of God bring life! Everlasting life! Salvation! Then Jesus went on to say to the woman: that well would spring up in those who believe in Him, into everlasting life! What does a fountain do? It sprays water up and out! Jesus is the Fountain, the Water of life and Jesus is the Word of life, and now we have the fountain of water, the words of life, to share with others!

Do you think Jesus explained the next thing He said to the woman at the well? The future place of worship? Not the temple in Jerusalem just for the Jews. Not on Mount Gerizim just for the Samaritans, but wherever people are! **"For where two or three are gathered together in My name, I am there in the midst of them."** (Matthew 18:20)

Whatever he said to them, many more believed Him, not just because of what she said; but they heard for themselves, and knew for themselves, that Jesus is the Christ, the Savior of the world!

We never hear of her in scripture again, but... the part of her life story that is in capital letters is: SHE FOUND THE MESSIAH AND SHE TOLD OTHERS!

That is the message she leaves us. If you believe Jesus can give you eternal life, don't you believe He can save others too? Should you be telling others?

If anyone thirsts, let him come to Me and drink.
(John 7:37)

FOOD FOR THOUGHT

1. Do you have the fountain of Living Water in you?
                    John 4:14

2. Do you share the Living Water, The Words of Life?
            Deuteronomy 6:4-9   Matthew 28:19-20
            2Corinthians 4:13   1Peter 3:15

3. When was the last time you shared the story and words of Jesus?

SONG   **WONDERFUL WORDS OF LIFE**

CHAPTER THIRTY-ONE

SAPPHIRIA

Acts 5:1-11

Every year, since the days of Moses, God's people celebrated Pentecost, the Feast of Weeks, at the end of the harvest. (Exodus 34:22) A time of consecration and sacrifice described in Leviticus 23:15-22 This was before there was even a city named Jerusalem.

Now, the Jews came to Jerusalem, their Holy city, every year for this celebration. The population of Jerusalem more than doubled during this time of feasting, celebration, sacrifices, being with family and renewing friendships from year to year. But this year something different happened.

There was a disturbance in the city. Something happened in the top story of one of the houses and people stopped in the street to see what it was about. Soon, there was a large crowd, and as the day worn on it became bigger and bigger!

God chose this Pentecost to bring Christ's kingdom to earth! On this day the church was born! And on this day, three thousand people became members of that church! (Acts 1&2)

Side note: These people were Jews and until that day, they were living under the Old Law, the Law of Moses. The day that law was given, fifteen hundred years before, three thousand people died because of their sins .

This day, the day the New Law was given, three thousand people were saved from their sins. And more every day!

The people had come from out of town and only planned on being there a few days, but now they didn't want to go home! They wanted to hear Peter preach another sermon. They wanted to meet and talk with the other apostles. They wanted to learn more about this new Way of living for God. But...they were running out of supplies and money.

The new believers who lived in Jerusalem were doing all they could to help the situation. They brought money to the apostles to distribute among those who needed help. Some of them even sold property or houses and gave the money to the apostles.

Ananias and Sapphira also sold a piece of land but they brought only part of the proceeds to the apostles.

Because the Holy Spirit was with him, Peter asked if this was all the money the land had sold for and Ananias said yes. Peter then asked him why he lied to the Holy Spirit. As long as he owned the land, it was his and when he sold it, the money was his to do as he wished.

Ananias immediately fell down dead and was carried out.

About three hours later, Sapphira came in, not knowing what had happened, and she told the same lie! Why did you and your husband agree to test the Holy Spirit, he asked her.

And she too fell down dead and was carried out!

Peter knew by the power of God that Sapphira and her husband lied! Why did they do this?

Did they want to impress Peter and the others by telling them, they gave all the proceeds? Did they really think they were impressing God? Did Sapphira and her husband want the applause, but were not willing to make the sacrifice?

No one told them, or ordered them to sell land and donate all the proceeds. We are not told they were not even asked to do it. We are not told the other people sold everything they owned and brought all the proceeds to the apostles! If they had sold everything they owned, they would have then been in need and become a burden just like those they were trying to help!

Surely Sapphira and her husband did not think they were impressing God with their false generosity! Or did they really believe God would not know the truth, but take their word for it?

Who were they trying to impress, the people or the Lord? Either way, Peter said **You have not lied to men, but to God.** (Acts 5:4) And they both paid the penalty.

What would Sapphira say to us today?

My lie cost me my physical life and my spiritual life. What will your lie cost you?

Lying lips are an abomination to the Lord, But those who deal truthfully are His delight. (Proverbs 12:22)

FOOD FOR THOUGHT

1. Sapphira and her husband did sell land and bring money to the apostles. So, was their lie a "half truth", or a "little lie" or a "white lie"? Is there is the difference in the kinds of lies? Do we ever lie to someone because we think it is the right thing to do at the time? What is the result when they find out? Have we hurt people with lies?

2. When we lie to someone else, does God take it personally?
   Proverbs 6:16-19   Proverbs 12:22   Proverbs 19:5
   Amos 2:4   Ezekiel 13:8   Revelation 21:8

3. Where do lies come from?
   John 8:44

SONG   IF I HAVE WOUNDED ANY SOUL

CHAPTER THIRTY-TWO

DORCAS-TABITHA

Acts 9:36-43

Dorcas lived in the Greek city of Joppa. We don't know anything about her family. Luke called her a disciple, a believer, a follower, a student of Christ.

We are told she was a blessing to those around her, by providing clothing to the widows and those in need. She used her means and time to care for others the best way she could do it, by using her talent to serve Christ.

Our good deeds are a sacrifice to the Lord. The fragrance of the things (money and supplies) which the church in Philippi sent to Paul, **were a sweet smelling aroma, an acceptable sacrifice, well pleasing to God.**(Philippians 4:18)

What was a sacrifice under the Old Law? A pure, white lamb, not crippled, not sick, not weak, not useless. The very best of the new flock! The most valuable lamb of the flock. Offered as a burnt offering, a sweet aroma to the Lord. If God's people were not obedient, He said He would not smell the sweet aroma of their sacrifices. (Leviticus 26:31)

So it is with our sacrifice, it should be the very best we have; something we wouldn't just give away for any other reason! Given from a pure heart. (good motives, purposes, for the right reasons)

A lot of people do good things, but for what purpose? Sometimes for a reward or recognition, or a pat on the back. "My glory" not to bring glory to God.

Dorcas **was full of Good works and charitable deeds which she did.** (Luke 9:36) A lot of people sit around and talk about something that needs to be done, or plan to do something. They talk about a need, a project, a solution, but they never get around to doing it. She did it!

There is old saying: "the road to perdition is paved with good intentions." We intend to do, we plan to do, we want to do. Dorcas did it!

God asked Moses, **"What is in your hand?"** Moses replied, **"A rod"**. (Exodus 4:2) A plain old rod, like every shepherd used to prod his sheep. God told him to use it! To serve and lead His people.

What was in the hand of Dorcas? A needle! What is in your hand? What is your talent? What are you good at? What do you enjoy doing? Find a way to use it for the Lord.

Dorcas gave of her time, her talent, her means (money) to buy the supplies needed for her sewing. It was a hard day for the church when Dorcas died, for the whole community.

Is it possible she died while working, sewing for the Lord? I have heard preachers say, the greatest honor would be to die in the pulpit. I have known of one that did. I have heard people say they would like to "go home" during worship services. I too, would like to leave while worshiping, studying, praying or working; serving the Lord, by caring for or teaching someone else.

When Dorcas died, the other disciples knew what to do. They sent for Peter! They had heard of, possibly even seen what he had done in Lydda. And he was still there, just five miles away! He had just healed a man who had been paralyzed for eight years! He could do something! (Acts 8:32-35)

Two men were sent to find Peter and they implored him to come immediately! When Peter arrived he found the room where Dorcas lay, full of the widows, grieving for their friend. He asked them them to leave him with the body, and when they had gone, he prayed and then told Tabitha to rise up! And she did! Did Peter raise her? No! Peter helped her from the bed and presented her alive. But he didn't raise her from the dead! The Lord did!

Why did this happen? Not only were the believers excited, but the whole community of Joppa! The story of Tabitha and her life was known, but now the people heard about the power of the Christ! And many believed! On the Lord Jesus! Not Peter. Peter did not bring glory to himself, but to the Lord!

We don't hear any more about Dorcas, but what an example she left us! Almost two thousand years later, we are still reading about her good works and charitable deeds.

Every time we read this account, Dorcas is telling us something. Are we listening? What is she saying to us?

Love the Lord! Serve Him by serving others!

Let your light so shine before men that they may see your good works and glorify your Father in heaven.
(Matthew 5:16)

FOOD FOR THOUGHT

1. Does your light shine? In your family? Your neighborhood? At your job? In your school? Do people see a difference in you?

    Matthew 5:14-16   1 Corinthians 4:6-7   1John 3:18

    Ephesians 5:8

2. Are you offering sacrifices to the Lord?

    Matthew 20:28   2Corinthians 2:15   1Peter 2:5

    Hebrews 13:16   Philippians 4:18

3. What does **to present our bodies a living sacrifice** mean? (Romans 12:1) To put ourselves at God's disposal; to always be ready to go whenever He needs us. To sacrifice what I want to do at any given time when I am needed to serve Him.

4. What are we told to do for others?

    Deuteronomy 15:11   Matthew 20:28   Matthew 25:35-40

    Luke 3:10-11   Galatians 6:10   Hebrews 13:2

    James 2:14-26   1 John 3:17

SONG   I WANT TO BE A WORKER

CHAPTER THIRTY-THREE

MARY, MOTHER OF JOHN MARK

Acts 12

Luke told us King Herod was harassing the church, even to the point of killing James, the brother of John. Then he had Peter arrested, put in chains and kept under guard because he was also preaching Christ.

We are not told how long Peter was in prison, but the church was in constant prayer for him. The night before Peter was to appear before Herod, **an angel of the Lord stood by him, and a light shone in the prison; and he struck Peter on the side and raised him up** (Acts 12:7) Read that again. It sounds like the angel had to wake Peter up! Can you imagine? In prison, in chains, standing trial the next morning, possibly facing execution and he was sound asleep! The angel led him out of the cell, past the guards, out the prison gates and down a street. Then the angel was gone!

Peter went on through the dark streets to the house where the church was gathered praying for him. Christians are being harassed, put in prison, and murdered, and the woman of the house opens her door and invites the church in! And they are inside now, praying for Peter and his circumstances. Is that not just asking for trouble? What if Herod found out they were meeting in her house?

When Peter showed up at her door, the church was astonished! He told them to be quiet! Talk softly, so the neighbors don't hear. Prison officials will soon miss him and be looking for him, so he cannot stay. He wanted to tell them their prayers had been answered how the angel got him out of prison and he wanted them to get word to James, the brother of Jesus and the other Christians. And he slipped off into the night.

Her name was Mary. She had a son still living at home and she was responsible for his well being and his safety. Was she putting him at risk by having Christians in her home?

These few verses are all we know about her. But, these few verses tell us a lot about her! Her great faith! Her courage! Her love for the church!

Her son, John Mark became a missionary and traveled with Paul and Barnabas. Later he ministered to Paul when Paul was in a Roman prison. (2Timothy 4:11) He worked along side of Peter and Timothy (1Peter 5:13) And spent the rest of his life working for the church. Mary's son wrote the book of Mark for all generations to come, so we can read the story of Jesus.

When we read the story of his life, his courage, his strong faith and love for the church, then we know.... he really is his mother's son!

What a tribute to his mother, his life was! What an example she was for him, and for us! These few verses show her courage and faith in a time of great tribulation, knowing at any moment she could be the next one arrested because she believed in the Christ.

What is the message Mary leaves for us?

Do not be afraid to stand for Christ! Show your faith so others might be encouraged!

Be strong and of good courage, do not fear or be afraid of them, for the Lord your God, He is the One who goes with you. He will not leave you or forsake you.

(Deuteronomy 31:6)

FOOD FOR THOUGHT

1. Are you a faithful, active member of the church? Is your faith seen by the other members or are you just an observer? Does your life in the church encourage others to be stronger, more faithful?

   James 1:21-22   1Timothy 4:12

   Does this one apply only to young ministers? Timothy was probably in his mid-thirties at this time.

2. Have you ever been in a situation where you were embarrassed to talk about Jesus? Is there ever a time when talking about Him is out of place?

   Matthew 10:32   Luke 12:8-9.

3. Is your faith strong enough to confess Jesus Christ even if it meant going to jail? What if showing, confessing your faith endangered your children?

   Psalm 27:1   Psalm 118:5-9   Hebrews 10:32-39

SONG **LIVING BY FAITH**

CHAPTER THIRTY-FOUR

LYDIA

Acts 15:40-41   Acts 16:11-15,40

Our story begins with Paul, Silas, Timothy and Luke. They were traveling city to city checking on newly established churches and they were on their way to Asia when the Holy Spirit interrupted their journey and redirected them, not once, but twice. They were to go to Philippi; a colony of Rome. There were no Christians there, very few Jews and no synagogues. This was a place of false gods!

Do you think God had a reason for the Holy Spirit sending them to such a city?

We don't know how long the men were in the city before they heard about a group of women who went on each Sabbath day to the river side and had prayers . We do not know if these women were Jewish, or Greeks who had heard about the God of Israel, but they were keeping the Sabbath and the men went to join them. Among those women was Lydia.

Luke gives us a little bit of background on Lydia. She was from the city of Thyatira and she was a business woman, a seller of purple. The chemical balance in the water in the city of Thyatira, combined with a special dye produced a very unique, vibrant shade of purple that could not be made anywhere else in the world. A rare and costly fabric worn by the very wealthy. She was the company's representative in Philippi.

Luke also tells us she was a worshiper of God.

We are not told how many days or weeks passed between verses thirteen and fifteen of Acts chapter sixteen; enough time for the men to teach Lydia and her household about the Christ and His church and how they could be part of that church. And Luke says **The Lord opened her heart to heed the things spoken by Paul.** (Acts 16:14) She was willing to listen and God helped her to understand.

When you call upon Me and go and pray to Me, and I will listen to you. And you will seek Me and find Me, and when you search for Me with all your heart, I will be found by you, says the Lord. (Jeremiah 29:13-14)

Luke tell us about another man named Cornelius who was searching for God and Peter was sent to teach him. (Acts:10)

The secret of all this is the phrase "with all your heart". It is conditional. All your heart. Some people just want to hear "God loves me" and nothing else. Lydia's heart was open to learn everything Paul was teaching about salvation. There was time spent asking and answering questions. Teaching, searching the scriptures to see what the prophets had to say about the coming Messiah. And then to hear about when the Christ really came and to hear about the birth of the church. And then she and her household were baptized. How many people were in her household? Husband? Children? Parents? Servants? Employees? Remember, at this time, an employer provided living quarters for their employees a well as any servants

Seems to me, God heard her prayers and sent Paul and the others as an answer for her, just like He sent Peter as an answer to Cornelius.

This is not the end of her story!

She insisted the men stay in her house and while they were staying with her, they were out in the city teaching and preaching. People were listening and believing. The Roman people didn't like all the talk about just one God and drug them to the authorities! **These men, being Jews, exceedingly trouble our city. They teach customs which are not lawful for us, being Romans, to receive.** (Luke 16:20-21) What would that be?

We have dozens of gods to worship and the law said every one was to worship Caesar! Now these men say we are to worship just one God.

The people caused such a riot, the magistrates had Paul and Silas stripped and beaten and put into prison. For what? They were Jews! Teaching Jesus! Remember the first Christians were converted Jews and the Romans thought they were just another sect of Jews, and they hated all Jews!

And while they were in prison, they continued teaching and preaching! Even the jailer and his family were converted to Christ!

When Paul and Silas were released and went back to Lydia's house, what was her reaction? Look what your new religion has caused!! Go away! She couldn't afford to offend the Romans and put her household and her business in jeopardy! The Romans could have arrested her too! So what did she do?

She welcomed them back into her home!

The rest of the story

By the time Paul and his companions left Phillipi, there was a church meeting there! The first one in all of Europe! **When they** (Paul and Silas) **entered the house of Lydia and when they had seen the brethren, they encouraged them and departed.** (Acts 16:40)

What message would Lydia have for us?

Search for the truth and when you have found it, stand firm! Have courage! Don't worry about the necessities of this life!

Seek first the kingdom of God and His righteousness, and all these things shall be added to you (Matthew 6:33)

FOOD FOR THOUGHT

1. What does the phrase "with all your heart" mean?

2. Where do we need to look for God's truth?
Psalm 119:105, 133, 142, 151,

   John 8:3`-32   John 17:17   Romans 10:17
   Romans 15:4   Acts 17:11   2 Timothy 2:15

3. Are we to worship or pray to anything a man made from wood? Stone? Precious metal? Are we to worship another person?
   Exodus 20:4   Matthew 4:10   Acts 17:29

SONG   **TEACH ME THY WAY**

CHAPTER THIRTY-FIVE

EUNICE & LOIS

Acts 16:1-3   2 Timothy 1:3-5
2 Timothy 3:15

The first time we hear of Eunice, Luke wrote, **He** (Timothy) **was the son of a certain woman who believed, but his father was Greek** (a non-believer) (Acts 16:1-3)

The year was around A.D. 49, sixteen years after the death of Christ. She was living in Lystia, a Roman colony that was of Greek culture. The great temple of Zeus was in her city. In her city, like all cities in the Roman empire, Christians were being persecuted. Her name was Eunice. She was of Jewish descent, and she was a Christian, as was her mother, Lois. And she was the mother of Timothy.

Eunice and her mother had taught Timothy the Holy Scriptures since he was a child and now he was about sixteen, eighteen years old and other Christians in Lystia were speaking well of him. When the apostle Paul came through Lystia, he saw potential in young Timothy. What did Paul see in Timothy? A knowledge of the scriptures? A talent for speaking? A way of relating to other people? A strong faith? Whatever it was, Paul took him on his first missionary journey and Timothy spent the rest of his life as a missionary and local minister.

The next time we hear about Eunice, the year is A.D. 67, seventeen years later. Her son is the minister for the church in Ephesus and Timothy is is in mourning. Either his mother or his grandmother has just died. Paul wrote to Timothy and told him, he was praying for Timothy day and night! Paul said **he remembered with great joy, the genuine faith** (honest, true, real faith) **that is in you, which dwelt first in your grandmother, Lois and in your mother, Eunice.** (2 Timothy 1:5)

What a tribute Paul paid to Eunice! A woman born a Jew, and born again as a Christian, married to an unbeliever, living in a pagan city and raising her son to become a minister of the Gospel! A woman of genuine faith!

Her message is loud and clear!

No matter where you live or the circumstances of your life, teach your children about God and His Son, Jesus!

from childhood, you have known the Holy Scriptures.
(2Timothy 3:15)

FOOD FOR THOUGHT

1. I have heard parents say, I am going to leave their religion up to them when they get older. But, they put their children in day school and sports at age four. They insist their children learn those things.

    If you are, or if you hope to, raise children, what is your number one responsibility to them? Their education? Sports? The arts? Their friends? Their eternity?

    Joshua 24:15   Deuteronomy 11:18-21   Matthew 18:6
    1 Timothy 4:8 2   Timothy 3:15   Ephesians 6:4

2. Is it ever too early to begin teaching your children about God and His Son?

    When you rock them to sleep, what are you singing to them?

    Do you say prayers with them that they can understand?

    Do you have Bible story books with pictures for little ones and Bibles for the older ones?

SONG   **JESUS LOVES ME**

CHAPTER THIRTY-SIX

EUODIA AND SYNTYCHE

Philippians 4:2-3

While Paul was under house arrest in Rome, he received word of a problem in the church in Philippi. There were two women there, Euodia and Syntyche who had worked along side Paul to spread the gospel, but now, there was a problem. Paul wrote, **I implore Euodia and Syntyche to be of the same mind in the Lord.** (Philippians 4:2)

What was their disagreement about? We are not told and I believe there is a reason we are not told. IT MAKES NO DIFFERENCE WHAT THEIR DISAGREEMENT WAS ABOUT They were to get along and work together. Period!

If those women were anything like the women of today, it probably was not about what needed to be done, but how to do it and who is in charge. Some women get their feelings hurt and then start talking to other women about what happened. People began taking sides and then it all goes down hill from there. Does any work get accomplished? If so, is it done out of love or spite? Is it done to get a pat on the back, to show what a hard worker you are? Or is it done to show the world what God can accomplish?

Some women are timid, some are very outgoing. Some women are organizers, while others are workers. Some tend to be more bossy than others. If you get two of the same kind one group, there can be problems and nothing gets done. Paul said, get over your differences and work together.

We are given absolute, detailed instructions about how some things are to be done, but some of the commands we received in scriptures, just say do it. We are not told how to feed the hungry, just do it! We are not told how to care for widow or orphans, just do it! We are not told how to go into all the world, just do it! Just work it out and work together, with love and do it!

We never hear of Euodia and Syntyche again, but their story is in scripture for a reason.

What would be their message for us?

For some things we are to do, there is no right way or wrong way, as long as God gets the glory! But.....if you don't do it, then you have a real problem with God!

And whatever you do, do it heartily, as to the Lord and not to men. (Colossians 3:23)

FOOD FOR THOUGHT

1. Is there someone who you have trouble working with?
   Is it better to walk away, and just don't do anything?
   I Corinthians 1:10   James 4:17

2. What does love look like?
   1 Corinthians 13

3. What can we do to help the situation?
   Matthew 5:9   2 Corinthians 13:11   Romans 14:19
   James 3:5-18

SONG   **INSTRUMENTS OF YOUR PEACE**

CHAPTER THIRTY-SEVEN

PRISCILLA

Acts 18:1-21, 24-26   1 Corinthians 16:19
Romans 16:3-5   2 Timothy 4:19

We never read about Priscilla without her husband. Scripture tells us about "their trade" or "their home". From all we read, these two people were devoted to each other and the church. She and her husband, Aquila, were Roman citizens born in Pontus, of Jewish descent, living in Rome and they were tent makers by trade.

Let's back up a little before we begin her story.

The first Christ followers were converted Jews living in Jerusalem. Those Jews who did not follow "The Way" hated the Jews who did because they chose to no longer live under the Law of Moses. They hated the followers of Christ just like they hated Christ, Himself. The leaders of the Jews had Christ crucified thinking that would be the end of the new religion, but when that Pentecost morning came, everything changed! The Way, the church, Christians, grew and spread like wildfire! So, the leaders of the Jewish courts began hunting Christians, all throughout Judea; having them arrested or even put to death, and Christians began running for their lives! Some went to Rome.

By A.D. 49, about sixteen years after the death of Jesus, there were Christians meeting in Rome and unconverted Jews were again causing problems. The disruption eventually went beyond the Jewish community because Gentiles were also being converted! Things got so bad, the Roman Emperor, Claudius, ordered all Jews, no matter what their religion was, out of Rome! Even if they were Roman citizens!

Enter Priscilla and her husband, Aquila. They packed up their home and business and joined thousands of other Jews and left Rome. These two found their way to Corinth and that is where we meet them for the first time.

Luke tells us, shortly after they arrived, Paul found them there and came to them. (Acts 18:2) Paul was also a tent maker by trade and they hired him to work for them and as was the custom, Paul lived with them.

While Paul was with Priscilla and her husband, he was also teaching in the synagogue every week and converting people to Christ. The rulers of the synagogue finally told him they didn't want him there any more, so he left and went right next door, to the home of a man named Justus who was not a Jew, but he was a worshiper of God. Paul converted Justus and they began a school and guess what??? The leader of the synagogue, a man named Crispus was converted to Christ! And many other people were also baptized. For sixteen months Paul taught in the house of Justus, the church was growing and the Jews were more and more unhappy.

Finally the Jews had enough of Paul. They didn't want him teaching Christ, anywhere, to anyone. So, they took him to a Roman court before the proconsul (governor) Gallio. He listened to their charges and dismissed the case. This is a disagreement between you Jews over your religion. You take care of it.

The Greek population stepped in! Our courts won't stand up and punish these trouble making Jews, so we will! A vigilante mob! They took the new Jewish synagogue leader, named Sosthenes, and gave him a public beating!

After all this, Paul remained there a good while living with Priscilla and her husband, working together, teaching and growing the church.

When Paul finally decided to move on, Priscilla and Aquila went with him. But before they left, there was a church there in Corinth.

When the three friends arrived in Ephesus, Priscilla and Aquila asked Paul to stay with them, but he needed to be in Jerusalem, so they said their good byes.

After Paul had gone, Priscilla and her husband set up house keeping and opened their business. One day they heard about a preacher that had come to town. His name was Apollos and he was a really eloquent speaker! Smart, knew the scripture and was on fire for the Lord! So they went to hear him, and he was every thing they heard about him, but something wasn't quite right.

How many of us have heard, or heard about preachers just like Apollos, really great preachers, but something was not quite right?

Apollos had the faith part right. He had the living for God part right. The doing good, helping and teaching others part right. But, he was teaching the wrong baptism!

So, Priscilla and Aquila took him off by himself and **explained to him the way of God more accurately.** (Acts 18:26) (Acts 2:38, Acts 22:16) Because of Priscilla and Aquila, the preacher, Apollos became a very influential preacher for Christ!

The next time we see Priscilla, it is seven years, later and Paul had gone back to Ephesus and while there, he wrote a letter back to the church in Corinth. He told the church in Corinth, that the church in Ephesus was meeting in the house of their old friends, Priscilla and Aquila! (1 Corinthians 16:19) And Paul also told them about another man they knew who was now in Ephesus; Sosthenes, the synagogue leader who had been beaten. (1 Corinthians 1:1) and Paul called him our brother. A fellow Christian!

A year later, Paul wrote a letter to the church in Rome and Priscilla and Aquila were back home! Back in Rome! and they had their business up and running again. The church was growing and meeting in their home! (Romans 16:3-5)

In time, the church in Rome was going so fast, they were having an impact on the city! And this time, most of the members were Gentiles!

It was no long just a "Jewish religion". It was Christianity! But, part of the problem was, Christians refused to bow and worship the emperor and law said everyone had to. Christians worshiped one God, and the Romans worshiped many gods! Christians were living a clean, moral life and that was insult to the life of debauchery enjoyed by the Roman population. At this time, Nero was the emperor and he was psychotic and a paranoid. He was afraid of the growing Christian population and so began the great persecution. Christians were thrown into prison, fed to lions for the entrainment of Nero and the Romans. They were hung on poles and set on fire to provide "lamps" to light the streets of Rome.

Finally in A.D. 64, in a plot to get rid of all the Christians, Nero had fire set to his own city! Half of Rome burned to the ground and Nero blamed the Christians! The Roman army and other citizens began hunting Christians to kill or imprison them. Many packed up and left. Others, who had no money and no way to leave went into hiding.

Tradition tells us Priscilla and Aquila stayed behind as long as possible in order to help others escape. Finally, they were forced to leave as well.

In A.D. 67 Paul wrote his second letter to Timothy who was preaching in Ephesus. Paul had been arrested in Jerusalem and as a Roman citizen, he had appealed to Caesar. Now he was was in a Roman prison dungeon waiting for his execution. Guess who was back in Ephesus with Timothy? Paul sent greetings to his friends **Prisca and Aquila.** (2 Timothy 4:19)

That is the last we hear of Prisca. We followed her for about eighteen years A.D. 49-67 A friend of Paul, through good times and bad. A faithful Christian. A worker for the Lord.

What message would Prisca send to us?

Wherever you are, whatever your circumstances, walk in faith and never forsake the church of your Lord.

Be faithful unto death and I will give you the crown of life.
Revelation 2:10

FOOD FOR THOUGHT

1. Are you faithful to the church? Can your fellow Christians depend on you to be there? Do they know they can call on you for help?
   Matthew 25:40   3 John 5   Hebrew 10:24-26
   Colossians 1:23

2. Where do we get faith like Prisca?
   Romans 10:17   Ephesians 3:14-21

3. How do you show your faith?
   1Corinthians16:13   Colossian1:10-11   James 2:14-26

SONG   OH FOR A FAITH THAT WILL NOT SHRINK

CHAPTER THIRTY-EIGHT

THE UNNAMED MOTHER

Romans 16:13

I would love to sit and visit with this mother. What a story she could tell us! Luke tells us, her son was sent to school to study under Gamaliel (Acts 22:3) This was a well known, sought after teacher of the Law. A student had to be well prepared to sit at this man's feet and learn. Her family came from the tribe of Benjamin, and that carried some weight. Her son spoke Hebrew and Greek, knew the Law and was zealous toward God. He was on fire for God and he wanted nothing more than to serve God.

Don't you know she was proud of her son! She had great aspirations for him. Maybe one day he would sit on the Sanhedrin court, the ruling power of the Jewish nation!

What were her feelings when her son was breathing threats and murder against members the new religion that was teaching against that same Law, the Law of Moses? How dare Jews turn away from the Law of Moses!

Then the high priest of that court, gave her son letters to carry to other places to arrest followers of Christ, **whether men or women, he might bring them bound bring them bound to Jerusalem.** (Acts 9:1-2) He was doing everything he could to defend the Law of God and the Jewish way.

Her son, on special assignment to arrest the ungodly trouble makers! How proud she must have been!

Then she received the news.........Saul! Her son! He had become a follower of that same horrible religion! A Christian!!! And now he was called Paul!

The only time we read about this woman, Paul had written a letter to the church in Rome and at the end of his epistle, he sent greetings to several people. Some of the names are familiar to us through these studies, but then Paul wrote, **Greet Rufus chosen in the Lord, and his mother and mine.** (Romans 16:13) Paul's brother and his mother were members of the church in Rome! She had become a Christian!!

We are not told when she became follower of Christ, but you know she did a lot of praying for her son Paul, for his safety and well being. In his work for Christ, he underwent a lot of persecution, beatings, shipwrecks, attacks by robbers. Often homeless, nothing to eat and no place to rest. Enemies on all sides, Jews and Gentiles wanted him dead! (2 Corinthians 11:24-28)

One of the hardest things a follower of any religion can do, is to accept the possibility of being wrong. Their first reaction is, what about my family? My heritage? How can I leave what I have always known?

Paul and his mother made a complete, total turn around! They were baptized and became Christians and lived for Him.

Was she still living when Paul was put in a Roman prison dungeon and finally beheaded for the cause of Christ?

I wonder what her message to us would be?

When you find the truth, do not deny it! Accept it! Embrace it!

They received the word with all readiness, and searched the Scriptures daily to find out whether these things were so. Act 17:11

FOOD FOR THOUGHT

1. How can you know for sure if something is truth?
    > Romans 10:17   Acts 17:11
    > 2 Timothy 2:15-16   John 17:17

2. If you find the truth and decide to change, it could cost you! Friends even family.
    > Matthew 10:36-39   Luke 9:23-26

3. If you do decide to follow Jesus, you may need to endure some hard times but what will be the reward?
    > John 8:32   Matthew 5:12   James 1:12
    > 1 Corinthians 9:24-27   1 Thessalonians 2:19

SONG   I HAVE DECIDED TO FOLLOW JESUS

A FEW LAST WORDS

When we study the women of the Bible in chronological order, we see the story of God's family. We see the unfolding of His plan for His family, that culminated in the church of His Son as the way to salvation. We see the struggles and temptations of God's children under three dispensations of time and we see His power, His care and provision; and most of all, His everlasting love to help His children overcome!

God's message for us? Do not just read the stories, study the lives of these women. Learn from them! Learn to love Him, obey Him and serve Him. He wants us to listen to the message of His Son and find His way for our salvation.

As we were studying the stories of these women, were you listening for their messages? What one word resonates through all the pages? FAITH Every story showed a strong faith or a lack of faith.

Read again Hebrews chapter eleven. Each one of the people pictured there, not only had faith, they showed their faith. Because of their faith, they did something! They obeyed God. They served God. They publicly acknowledged God. They praised Him and they thanked Him.

If Moses' mother believed in God, but chose to obey Pharoah, what would have happened?

If Rahab believed in God but changed her mind and had not helped the Israelites, what would have happened?

If Mary believed in God, but refused to be the mother of His Son, what would have happened?

My husband, Mike has a favorite saying: It is one thing to BELIEVE IN GOD and another thing to BELIEVE GOD.

If I believe there is a God, but I do not believe what He says; instead, I choose not to love, listen, serve, worship and obey Him, what will be the outcome for me?

Now lets read the first two verses of the next chapter of Hebrews. We are told, now that we have all these examples, the heroes listed above, we are to lay aside the things that tempt us and the sins we indulge in and follow their examples: get busy, and live a life of active faith. The writer calls our lives **the race that is set before us looking unto Jesus, the author and finisher of our faith.** (Hebrews 12:1-2) A race has a beginning and an end. The starting point is the day we are baptized into Jesus for the remission of our sins. The finish line is our death! Jesus, through His death and resurrection, was the maker of this plan; of living a life of obedient faith. **Without faith it is impossible to please Him, for he who comes to God must believe that He is and that He is the rewarder of those who diligently seek Him.** (Hebrews 11:6)

James, the brother of Jesus tells us, not once, but six times, faith without works is dead. Faith alone will not save us. Works alone will not save us.... but works produced by faith justifies us.

Our faith brings us to love the Lord God and His Son. Our faith brings us to obedience and baptism for the remission of our sins. Our faith brings us to good works. All of this results in our salvation.

One last song, my mother's favorite. She said it told the whole story of her faith, everything she believed.

WE SAW THEE NOT

My prayer for you is: May your life be a reflection of the woman of Proverbs 31 and may the fruit of the Spirit be seen in you. May God bless you as you walk through His creation showing your faith to all those around you.

Jean

LIST OF WOMEN
IN THE BIBLE

1. ABI - daughter of Zechariah, wife of Ahaz and mother of Hezekiah   2 Kin 18:1-2
   also called ABIJAH   2 Chr 29:1
2. ABIGAIL #1 - wife of Nabal, later wife of King David   1 Sam 25:3,42
3. ABIGAIL #2 - sister of King David   1 Chr 2:13-16
4. ABIHAIL #1 - wife of Abishur   1 Ch 2:29
5. ABIHAIL #2 - wife of King Rehoboam   2 Chr 11:18
6. ABIJAH #1 - wife of Hezron   1 Chr 2:24
7. ABIJAH #2 – wife of Ahaz   2 Chr 28:27
   mother of Hezekiah also called Abi   2 Chr 29:1
8. ABISHAG - a servant of King David   1 Kin1-3-4
9. ABITAL - wife of King David   1 Chr 3:3
10. ACHSAH – daughter of Caleb   Josh 15:16-17
11. ADAH #1 – wife of Lemech   Gen 4:19
12. ADAH #2 – daughter of Elon, wife of Esau   Gen 36:2
13. AHINOAM #1 – wife of King Saul   1 Sam 14:50
14. AHINOAM #2 – wife of King David   1 Sam 25:43
15. AHLAI – daughter of Sheshan   1 Chr 2:31,34
16. AHOLIBAMAH – wife of Esau   Gen 36:2
17. ANAH – daughter of Zibeon   Gen 36:2
18. ANNA - the prophetess   Luke 2:36-38
19. APPHIA – member of the church in Colosse   Philem 2
20. ASENATH -wife of Joseph   Gen 41:45
21. ATARAH – wife of Jerahmeel   1 Chr 2:26
22. ATHALIAH – Queen of Judah   2 Chr 22:2-12

23. AZUBAH #1 – wife of Caleb	1 Chr 2:18-19
24. AZUBAH #2 – wife of King Asa	1 Kin 22:42
25. BAARA – wife of Shaharaim	1 Chr 8:8
26. BASEMETH#1 - wife of Esau, daughter of Elon	Gen 26:34
27. BASEMETH #2 – daughter of Ishmael	Gen 36:3
28. BASEMETH #3 – daughter of Solomon	1 Kin 4:15
29. BATHSHEBA – wife of King David, mother of Solomon	2 Sam 12:24
also spelled BATHSHUA	1 Chr 3:5
30. BITHIAH – daughter of Pharaoh	1 Chr 4:18
31. BERNICE -daughter of King Agrippa I and sister of	Acts 25:13
King Agripopa 2	
32. BILHAH – concubine of Jacob	Gen 30:1-3
33. BITHIAH – daughter of Jacob	1 Chr 4:18
34. CANDACE – Queen of Ethopia	Acts 8:27
35. CHLOA – member of the church in Corinth	1 Cor 1:11
36. CLAUDIA – member of the church in Ephesus	2 Tim 4:21
37. COZBI – a Midianite princess	Numbers 25:15, 31:8
38. DAMARIS – a woman converted by Paul	Acts 17:34
39. DEBORAH #1 – Rebekah"s nursemaid	Gen 35:8
40. DEBORAH #2 – prophetess and judge	Judg 4:4
41. DELILAH – a woman who betrayed Samson	Judg 16:12
42. DINAH – daughter of Jacob	Gen 30:17,21
43. DRUSILLA – wife of Felix	Acts 24:24
44. DORCAS - a disciple of Jesus,	Acts 9:36
45. EGLAH – wife of King David	2 Sam 3:5
46. ELISHEBA – wife of Aaron	Ex 6:23
47. ELIZABETH – mother of John the baptizer	Luke 1:13
48. EPHAH – concubine of Caleb	1 Chr 2:46
49. EPHRATH – wife of Caleb, mother of Hur	1 Chr 2:19
also spelled EPHRATHAH	1 Chr 2:50
50. ESTHER – Queen of the Persian Empire	Book of Esther
also called HADASSAH	Esther 2:7
51. EUNICE – mother of Timothy	2 Tim 1:5
52. EUODIA – member of the church in Philippi	Philipp 4:2

53. EVE – first woman	Gen 3:20
54. GOMER – wife of Hosea	Hos.1:2-3
55. HAGAR – wife of Abraham	Gen 16:3
56. HAGGITH - wife of King David	2 Sam 3:4
57. HAMMOLEKHETH – granddaughter of Manasseh	1 Chr. 7:17
58. HAMUTAL – wife of King Josiah and mother of King Jehoahaz	2 Kin 23:30,31
59. HANNAH – wife of Elkanah and mother of Samuel	1 Sam 1:5,20
60. HAZZELELPONI – daughter 0f Etham	1 Chr 4:3
61. HELAH – wife of Ashur	1 Chr 4:5
62. HEPHZIBA – mother of Manasseh	2 Kin 21:1
63. HERODIAS – wife of King Herod and his brother Philip	Mark 6:17
64. HODESH – wife of Shaharaim	1 Chr 8:8-9
65. HOGLAH - -daughter of Zelophehad	Num 26:33
66. HULDA – prophetess of God	2 Kin 22:15-17
67. HUSHIM – wife of Shaharaim	1 Chr 8:8
68. ISCAH – daughter of Haran	Gen 11:29
69. JAEL – wife of Heber	Jud 4:17
70. JECHOLIAH – King Uzziah	2 Chr 26:3
also called Azariah	2 Kin15:2
71. JEDIDAH – mother of King Josiah	2 Kin 22:1
72. JEHOADDAH #1 – daughter of Ahaz, mother of Alemeth, Azmaveth and Zimri	1 Chr.8:36
also called JARAH	1 Chr. 9:42
73. JEHOADDAN #2 – wife of Jehoahaz, King of Israel mother of King Amaziah	2 Kin 14:2
74. JEHOSHEBA – daughter of King Joram	2 Kin 11:2
75. JEHUDIJAH – mother of Jered	1 Chr 4:18
76. JEMIMAH – daughter of Job	Job 42:14
77. JERIOTH – wife of Caleb	1 Chr 2:18
78. JERUSHA – wife of King Uzziah, daughter of Zadok	2 Kin 15:32-33
also spelled JERUSHAH	2 Chr 27:1
79. JEZEBEL – wife of King Ahab	1 Kin 16:31
also called the false prophetess	Rev 2:20
80. JOANNA – supported the ministry of Jesus	Luke 8:3

81. JOCHEBED – mother of Moses .... Ex 6:20

82. JUDITH – wife of Esau .... Gen 26:34

83. JULIA – member of the church in Rome .... Rom 16:15

84. JUNIA – Relative of Paul in Rome and a fellow prisoner .... Rom 16:17

85. KEREN-HAPPUCH – daughter of Job .... Job 42:14

86. KETURAH – wife of Abraham .... Genesis 25:1

87. KEZIAH - daughter of Job .... Job 42:14

88. LEAH – wife of Jacob .... Gen 29:23-27

89. LOIS – grandmother of Timothy .... 2 Tim 1:5

90. LO-RUHAMAH – daughter of Hosea .... Hosea 1:6

91. LYDIA – first European Christian .... Acts 16:14-15

92. MAACAH – wife of King David, mother of Absalom .... 2 Sam 3:3

93. MAACHAH #1- daughter of Nahor .... Gen 22:20-24

94. MAACHAH #2 – concubine of Calab .... 1 Chr 2:48

95. MAACHAH #3 – wife of Machir .... 1 Chr 7:15

96. MAACHAH #4 – granddaughter of Absalom, wife of Rehoboam
    mother of Jeush, Shamariah and Zaham .... 1 Chr 11:18-21

97. MAACHAH #5 – granddaughter of Absalom, wife of Jeroboam
    mother of Nebat, grandmother of Asa .... 1 Kin 15:2

98. MAHALATH #1 – daughter of Ishmael, wife of Esau .... Gen 28:9

99. MAHALATH #2 – granddaughter of David, wife of Rehoboam .... 2 Chr 11:18

100. MAHLAH #1 – daughter of Zelophehad .... Numbers 26:33

101. MAHLAH #2 – daughter of Hammoleketh .... 1 Chr 7:18

102. MARTHA - sister of Mary .... John 11:1-2

103. MARY – mother of Jesus, James, Joses, Judas and Simon .... Mark 6:1-3

104. MARY – mother of John Mark .... Acts 12:12-17

105. MARY – sister of Martha .... John 11:1-2

106. MARY – wife of Cleophas .... John 19:25

107. MARY – member of the church in Rome .... Rom 16:6

108. MARY MAGDALENE – follow of Jesus .... Matt 27:56

109. MATRED – daughter of Mezahab .... Gen 36:39

110. MEDIUM OF ENDOR – visited by King Saul .... 1 Sam 28:3-25

111. MEHETABLE – daughter of Matred, wife of Hadar .... Gen 36:39

112. MERAB – daughter of King Saul .... 1 Sam 14:49

113. MESHULLEMETH – wife of King Manasseh .... 2 Kin 21:18-19

114. MEZAHAB – mother of Matred	Gen 36:39
115. MICHAL - daughter of King Saul	1 Sam 14:49
116. MICHAIAH – mother of King Jeroboam	2 Chr 13:1-2
117. MILCAH #1 – daughter of Haran, wife of Nahor	Gen 11:29
118. MILCAH #2 – wife of King Dsavid	1 Sam 18:20-21
119. MILCAH #3 – daughter of Zelophehad	Num 26:32
120. MIRIAM #1 – sister of Moses	Num 26:59
121. MIRIAM #2 – daughter of Mered	1 Ch 4:17
122. NAAMAH #1 – daughter of Lamech, sister of Tubal -Cain	Gen 4:19-22
123. NAAMAH #2 – wife of King Solomon	I Kin 14:21
124. NAOMI – mother-in-law of Ruth	Ruth 1:4
also called Mara	Ruth 1:20
125. NEHUSHTA – mother of King Jechoiachin	2 Kin 24:8
126. NOADIAH – a prophetess	Neh 6:14
127. NOAH – daughter of Zelophehad	Num 26:33
128. ORPAH – Ruth's sister-in-law	Ruth 1:4
129. PENINNAH – wife of Elkanah	1 Sam 1:2-4
130. PERSIS – member of the church in Rome	Rom 16:12
131. PHOEBE – member of the church in Cenchrea	Rom 16:1
132. PRISCILLA – wife of Aquilla	Acts 18:1-3
also called Prisca, by Paul	2 Tim 4:19
133. PUAH – a Hebrew midwife in Egypt	Ex 1:15
134. RACHEL – wife of Jacob, mother of Joseph	Gen 29:22
135. RAHAB – a harlot of Jericho	Josh 2:1
136. REBEKAH – wife of Isaac	Gen 24:67
137. REUMAH – concubine of Nahor	Gen 22:24
138. RHODA – a Christian in Jerusalem	Acts 12:13
139. RIZPAH – a concubine of King Saul	2 Sam.3:6-8
140. RUTH – daughter-in-0law of Naomi	Ruth 1:2-4
141. SALOME – sister of Mary John 19:25	Mark 15:40-41
142. SAPPHIRIA – proved herself a liar	Acts 5:1-11
143. SARAI – wife of Abraham, God renamed her SARAH	Gen 17:15
144. SERAH – daughter of Asher	1Chr 7:30
145. SHEERAH – founder of three towns	1 Chr 7:24
146. SHELOMITH #1 – mother of a blasphemer	Lev 24:11

147. SHELOMITH #2 – daughter of Zerubbabel	1 Chr 3:19
148. SHELOMITH #3 – daughter of Rehoboam	2 Chr 11:18-20
149. SHIMEATH – an Ammoritess, conspired against King Joash	2 Chr 24:24-26
150. SHIMRITH – a Moabitess, conspired against King Joash	2 Chr 24:24-26
151. SHIPHRAH – a Hebrew midwife in Egypt	Ex 1:15
152. SHUA #1 – mother of three of Judah's sons	1 Chr 2:3
153. SHUA #2 –daughter of Heber	1 Chr 7:32
154. SUSANA – follower of Jesus	Luke 8:23
155. SYNTYCHE – a member of the church in Philippi	Phil 4:2
156. TABITHA – see Dorcas	
157. TAHPENES – Egyptian queen	1 Kin 11:19-20
158. TAMAR #1 – daughter-in-law of Judah	Gen 38:6
159. TAMAR #2 – daughter of King David, sister of Absalom	2 Sam 13:1
160. TAPHATH – daughter of Solomon	1 Kin 4:11
161. TIMNA – concubine of Eliphaz	Gen 36:12
162. TIRZAH – daughter of Zelophehad	Num 26:33
163. TRYPHANA – worker in the church in Rome	Rom 16:12
164. TRYPHOSA – worker in the church in Rome	Rom 16:12
165. VASHTI – wife of King Ahasueaus	Esther 1:9
166. ZEBUDAH – mother of King Jehoiakim	2 Kin 23:36
167. ZILLAH – wife of Lamech	Gen 4:19

There may be more that I did not find and there are many more unnamed women in Scripture. A lot of women are only mentioned as a family connection.

BIOGRAPHY

Jean taught her first Bible class at age sixteen and has never stopped. She majored in English at Idaho State University and Magic Valley Christian College. Since then she has worn many hats; teacher, artist, wife, mother, florist, co-owner of "I Do" Weddings, grandmother, gardener, bride for the second time and great grandmother.

She has taught in Bible classes and Bible camps across the U.S., in Africa, Mexico and Ukraine.

She and her husband, Mike live on three and a half acres in the beautiful Hot Springs area of Arkansas and spend time working outside and enjoying the beauty god gave them.

They work and worship with the Village Church of Christ and are living a blessed life.

Printed in the United States
by Baker & Taylor Publisher Services